Confession:
The
Sacrament
of
Mercy

PONTIFICAL COUNCIL FOR THE PROMOTION
OF THE NEW EVANGELIZATION

Jubilee of Mercy
2015-2016

Our Sunday Visitor Publishing Division
Our Sunday Visitor, Inc.
Huntington, Indiana 46750

Copyright © 2015 Pontifical Council for the Promotion of the New Evangelization Vatican City

Published 2015 by Our Sunday Visitor Publishing Division

20 19 18 17 16 15   2 3 4 5 6 7 8 9

Our Sunday Visitor Publishing Division, Our Sunday Visitor, Inc., 200 Noll Plaza, Huntington, IN 46750; 1-800-348-2440

ISBN: 978-1-61278-982-8 (Inventory No. T1742)
eISBN: 978-1-61278-990-3
LCCN: 2015948494

Translation: Damian Bacich
Cover design: Lindsey Riesen
Cover art: Shutterstock; Pontifical Council for the Promotion of the New Evangelization
Interior design: Sherri Hoffman

PRINTED IN THE UNITED STATES OF AMERICA

TABLE OF CONTENTS

Introduction. 5

CHAPTER ONE: Jesus' Forgiveness of Sins. 7
   1. A Controversial Subject / 7
     Losing the Meaning of Forgiveness / 10
     The Wonder of Experience / 11
   2. An Event both Ecclesial and Personal / 14
     The Faith of the Four Stretcher-Bearers / 16
     Rise and Go Home / 18

CHAPTER TWO: A Father and Two Sons 21
   1. A Son's Return / 21
     The Experience of Sin / 23
     The Experience of Forgiveness / 26
   2. Entering the Father's House? / 27
     The Mentality of a Hired Servant / 29
     Accepting the Invitation / 30
   3. A Father's Compassion / 30
     The Gifts of Mercy / 32
     The Feast of Forgiveness / 34

CHAPTER THREE: Of Debts and Debtors 37
   1. The Parable of the Good King and the
     Unforgiving Servant / 38
     A Crippling Debt / 39

Settling Accounts / 40

The Final Judgment / 41

2. Forgive Us Our Debts / 43

3. We Forgive Our Debtors / 44

CHAPTER FOUR: The Gift of the Spirit and Forgiveness

of Sins 47

CHAPTER FIVE: The Words of Forgiveness 53

God the Father of Mercies Has Reconciled the World

to Himself / 53

In the Death and Resurrection of His Son / 55

And He Sent the Holy Spirit for the Remission of Sins / 57

Through the Ministry of the Church / 59

Pardon and Peace / 62

And I Absolve You from Your Sins in the Name of

the Father and of the Son and of the Holy Spirit / 63

CHAPTER SIX: The Sacrament of Reconciliation in Pastoral

Ministry 65

1. The Formation of Conscience / 66

2. Educating to the Meaning of Penance / 69

3. Living Reconciliation / 72

Reconciliation Within the Community / 75

a) Seeking Out the Missing / 75

b) Brotherly Correction / 76

Architects of Reconciliation in the World / 78

INTRODUCTION

In calling for an extraordinary jubilee year centered on the mercy of God, Pope Francis characterized it as "a new stage in the journey of the Church on its mission to bring to every person the Gospel of mercy." He then added, "I am convinced that the whole Church will find in this Jubilee the joy needed to rediscover and make fruitful the mercy of God, with which all of us are called to give consolation to every man and woman of our time" (Homily at St. Peter's Basilica, March 13, 2015).

Seeking to offer a contribution in response to such expectations and recalling that "the Gospel is the revelation in Jesus Christ of God's mercy to sinners" (*Catechism of the Catholic Church*, 1846), we offer some reflections in order to better understand the sacrament of confession, the sacrament of those who, in Christ, experience the merciful love of God. The style of the first four chapters is splendidly biblical. The argumentation is based on four passages, one for each Gospel, in which the themes of mercy, forgiveness of sins, and conversion are placed by Jesus at the center of his teaching and action. In the subsequent chapters, what prevails instead is a more systematic and pastoral reflection in support of a more coherent understanding of the sacrament.

Today it is rather common to draw attention to the widespread disaffection with the practice of confession. The reasons have been pointed out many times, from the denial of its usefulness to the conviction that forgiveness is a purely private affair between one's conscience and God. There are also those who feel uncomfortable confessing their sins to a priest, while others complain about their disappointment at the unavailability of priests and well-prepared confessors. Perhaps it is necessary to recognize that the difficulty in approaching the sacrament of confession is also a mirror of the difficulty in placing one's faith in God and, above all, in his mercy. This Jubilee can be a privileged moment for re-proposing, as a central theme of pastoral ministry, the Sacrament of Reconciliation in a way that captures its beauty and effectiveness.

The Pontifical Council for the Promotion of the New Evangelization is profoundly grateful to Father Maurizio Compiani who dedicated himself to authoring these pages with competence and pastoral sensitivity. Our wish is that reading and reflecting on this pastoral instrument may allow you to grasp God's joy at forgiving and the power of mercy as a sign of his closeness and tenderness.

✠ Rino Fisichella
President, Pontifical Council for the
Promotion of the New Evangelization

CHAPTER 1

Jesus' Forgiveness of Sins

In the chapter titled "The Sacraments of Healing," the *Catechism of the Catholic Church* deals with the Sacrament of Reconciliation (1420-98). The argumentation is framed by two evangelical statements, one at the beginning of the section, and the other near the conclusion, regarding the paralytic healed by Jesus at Capernaum (see Mk 2:1-12). In this circumstance, a debate breaks out between Jesus and the scribes on the subject of the forgiveness of sins. We therefore begin our reflection with this episode.

1. A Controversial Subject

The fact that the subject of the forgiveness of sins has always caused embarrassment and raised difficulties is already attested to in Mark's Gospel, which is the earliest. It is significant that the first controversy, indeed provoked by Jesus himself, has to do with the forgiveness of sins.

From Scandal

At Capernaum, Jesus addresses a paralytic brought to him, "Child, your sins are forgiven" (2:5). These words scandalize some of the scribes present, who object in their hearts: "Why does this man speak like this? It is blasphemy! Who can forgive sins but God alone?"

(v. 7). Considered blasphemous, Jesus' words provoke bewilderment and contempt in the doctors of the law. Their strong reaction is, however, comprehensible if it is compared to the teachings of the Hebrew tradition. Forgiveness of sins, in fact, was considered the exclusive privilege of God alone! ("I am He who blots out your transgressions for my own sake, and I will not remember your sins," Is 43:25.) God would certainly manifest it during the messianic era, since his salvation of his people would also include the forgiveness of sins ("Who is a God like you, pardoning iniquity / and passing over transgression / for the remnant of his inheritance? / He does not retain his anger for ever / because he delights in mercy. / He will again have compassion upon us, / he will tread our iniquities under foot. / You will cast all our sins / into the depths of the sea," Mi 7:18-19.)

And yet, despite the fact that expectations for the Messiah were numerous and varied (a liberator from foreign occupation, the one who would gather together the people that had been dispersed, the faithful interpreter of the Law), no one had ever dared attribute to God's Anointed One the power to forgive anyone's sins. Such a thing was an absolute prerogative of God, the One! In judging Jesus' words to be blasphemy, the scribes show themselves to have a lucid awareness of man's condition on earth and the nature of authentic religious experience. They actually take seriously the abyss that separates man, by his nature a sinner, from God who is thrice holy (see Is 6:3). Between the bursting forth of the life of God and the fragility of his own existence, man recognizes a tremendous gap and realizes that he is unworthy of entering into a relationship with him. No man can bridge such a distance. Only God can take the initiative and forgive sins, reconciling the sinner to himself and opening up the possibility of communion with him.

Biblical tradition had therefore strictly tied the forgiveness of sins to worship, the sacred space in which God's power acts by means of a sacrificial rite, in which the priest offered the expiatory victim (see Lv 4-5), or else by means of the solemn and complex liturgy of the day of atonement, Yom Kippur (Ex 30:10; Lv 23:26-32). In harmony with the biblical texts, the scribes attributed to God alone the role of agent of salvation. Consequently, to their ears Jesus' words to the paralytic are unacceptable and unbearable, since they seem to be aimed at deceiving him about his condition and above all position their speaker at the level of the "one" God of Israel.

To Wonder

The paralytic's miraculous healing stirs up a new reaction in all those present, which this time manifests itself openly. The crowd is beside itself with wonder and praises God, saying, "We never saw anything like this!" (v. 12). In Jesus' words about forgiveness and in the sudden healing of the paralytic, the crowd recognizes the unique relationship uniting Jesus with God. In Jesus' works, healing and forgiving sins are two closely related aspects, since they attest to his power to reconcile people to God by healing their relationships with him. Contrary to the scribes, the crowd resolves the controversy with a judgment in Jesus' favor. "We never saw anything like this," an authority whose power caused a pallet-bound paralytic to walk, just as they had never seen an authority with the power to forgive sins here "on earth."

In every time period, the Church's evangelizing mission causes scandal and wonder. Indeed the Church, by the Lord's mandate, never tires of announcing the Gospel, "the power of God for salvation to every one who has faith" (Rom 1:16), and ceaselessly reminding everyone that in Jesus Christ "we have redemption through his blood, the forgiveness of our trespasses, according to the riches of his grace" (Eph 1:7). Even today the same reactions provoke the community of believers and pose a question to society as a whole: Who can forgive sins? And at a more basic level, do terms such as "sin," "forgiveness," "mercy", "reconciliation" have a place in the world we are building? Do we still have need of forgiveness, of God's forgiveness? Is there still space for the experience of mercy?

Losing the Meaning of Forgiveness

When society exalts the individual to the point of placing him in continuous competition with others, and at all costs, the very concepts of "forgiveness" and "salvation" become incomprehensible and intolerable. For what do we need to be forgiven? And why do we need to be saved? The mirage of human omnipotence that technological progress seems to inspire — the quest for the myth of eternal youth, ostentatious well-being, efficiency and productivity as the only social criteria that matter — all lead to an alienated and alienating vision of man and of life. Within this vision all boundaries are broken and destroyed. Limits per se, even the most natural and ethical, are considered "evil" by the simple fact that they impede the quest for freedom without any reference points other than the affirmation of oneself over and against everyone and everything.

So confessing our sin sounds like weakness and invoking God's forgiveness seems like a humiliating rite to leave behind. We no longer believe in God's mercy because we are no longer aware of sin, and we no longer have a sense of sin because within us there is the underlying conviction that there is no objective notion of good and evil. This *limitless ego* is opposed to any recognition of guilt, since its every decision and action only has self-referential criteria. Thus our perception of ourselves, of the world, of others, and of God becomes sinister and hostile. The *limitless ego* becomes the *alienated and selfish ego*. In a world of perfection, for a society of individuals who wish to be perfect, to recognize themselves as sinners who need to be saved is always a scandal. "The call to conversion as the indispensable condition of Christian love is particularly important in contemporary society, where the very foundations of an ethically correct vision of human existence often seem to have been lost" (St. John Paul II, *Tertio Millennio Adveniente*, 50). Christ's command to his disciples to go into the whole world and preach the Gospel is therefore more urgent than ever — the Gospel of Truth and of Salvation, the Gospel that enkindles faith, that incites conversion and illuminates life by unmasking every false vision of man and of society.

As Pope Francis reminds us:

> There is an urgent need, then, to see once again that faith is a light, for once the flame of faith dies out, all other lights begin to dim. The light of faith is unique, since it is capable of illuminating every aspect of human existence. A light this powerful cannot come from ourselves but from a more primordial source: in a word, it must come from God. Faith is born of an encounter with the living God who calls us and reveals his love, a love which precedes us and upon which we can lean for security and for building our lives. Transformed by this love, we gain fresh vision, new eyes to see; we realize that it contains a great promise of fulfillment, and that a vision of the future opens up before us. (*Lumen Fidei*, 4)

The Wonder of Experience

When forgiveness of sin becomes "experience," scandal gives way to wonder. In the Sacrament of Reconciliation, the good news about the forgiveness of sins becomes a certainty, and the sinner is reached by God's mercy and is regenerated by a grace that has multiple characteristics.

First of all it is an *experience of something freely given*. No one has sufficient merit to demand pardon, because God's *for-giveness* cannot be taken, but only implored and received. It is, in fact a *gift* that reaches man through Christ. In pronouncing the words of forgiveness on the cross (see Lk 23:34), the Anointed One of God not only shows the meaning of his death, but he makes the Father's mercy shine through him. In Jesus crucified and risen, all is forgiven us! And this free gift enkindles gratitude.

The forgiveness of sins is an *experience of light*. The mercy with which God reaches the sinner is not a vague feeling that defines our goodness, but the firm determination with which he effectively extends the salvation that Christ achieved on the cross to each and every one of us in a complete and definitive way. This means that only the Crucified and Risen One is the acceptable center of compassion for man, for history, and for the world. It other words, he is the standpoint from which each and every person can discover the meaning of God's plan for himself and for the world, the value of his actions and meaning of death. In receiving the remission of sins, we are thereby enlightened regarding the heart of God and his will. In the face of God, we discover the face of a Father who never gives up on any of his children.

The forgiveness of sins is an *experience of truth*. By continuing to implore God for forgiveness, the Christian keeps his own conscience alert to the truth of his condition as a sinner. Indeed, one of the greatest risks that a disciple of Jesus can run into is to no longer know how to gauge the depth and gravity of this condition. For a Christian, sin and the evil that results from it are not simply breaking a law, but a reality that penetrates and surrounds him without ever being able to fully understand its roots and consequences. Evil never openly proclaims itself beforehand, but it adapts itself and hides in the secret folds of the most banal and daily human life. Only a particularly sharp eye can discern it before it explodes in all its horrible reality. After all, history and experience teach us that intending to do good is not enough to avoid evil — terrible crimes have been committed by those convinced they were pursuing good. The Sacrament of Reconciliation attests to the fact that there is clearly a mystery of evil that surpasses us, and toward which we should cultivate a cautious, humble, and lucidly prudent attitude, without the illusion of ever having fully understood and overcome it with only our reason and good will.

In the Christian perspective, the Cross of Christ, from which the Father's mercy flows, reveals in all its drama the reality of our sin and our sinful state because, whether we know it or not, what we are capable of becomes clear on the cross. Without explicitly willing it, we are capable of killing God himself. Thus the crucifix becomes a permanent testimony to our radical blindness and powerlessness in the face of evil and sin, so much so that without Christ we would be radically and definitively lost. So the light that the crucifix sheds on the mystery of evil goes to the root of any presumptuous claim to truly and deeply know ourselves, to know who we really are.

The forgiveness of sins is an experience of regeneration that renews the grace of baptism and consecrates one's personal and ecclesial path of conversion as a commitment that is continually renewed. Reconciling with God transfigures the Christian sinner, renews his strength, and reintroduces him to the fulfillment of his mission in the Church and in the world. For the believer, the Sacrament of Reconciliation is a sacrament of healing that accompanies him in following Christ, by supporting him on the journey marked by his fragility and weakness.

The forgiveness of sins is an *experience of communion*. The forgiveness that God offers the sinner is never a purely individualistic phenomenon. Just as the call to faith implies a personal response but also inserts the believer into a community of disciples, God's forgiveness takes place not only in the depths of the heart but is received through the Church and within her bosom. Reconciliation to God strengthens the communion of the community of believers. Indeed, it is from God's love that reached us in Christ that the Christian learns how to love. God's overabundant grace is poured out again upon the brethren. Thus the "I" of the believer is inseparable from the "we" of the community, and God's forgiveness, given in Christ through the Holy Spirit, unites everyone in one sole mystery of communion.

Finally, the forgiveness of sins is *an experience of wonder.* Precisely because it is "in Christ," the revelation of sin and of its individual and collective mystery can never become separated from the salvation that he offers us, because the Crucified One is also the Resurrected One. Consequently, even while looking into the abyss of evil that surrounds us and penetrates us, Christians are not afraid of becoming aware of our own personal sins and openly confessing them, because we are always on the move. Our point of departure is a fundamental certainty of salvation already offered, like a friendly hand that guided us through a minefield we recognized only after successfully navigating it. The wonder of recognition necessarily accompanies such awareness, a wonder in which confession of sins, salvation freely given, and an outpouring of love all join together, and where the free nature of that gift becomes abundantly clear.

As Pope Benedict XVI recalled:

> The Sacrament of Reconciliation, which begins with a look at one's actual condition in life, contributes uniquely to achieving that "openness of heart" which enables one to turn one's gaze to God so that he may enter one's life. The certainty that he is close and in his mercy awaits the human being, even one who is involved in sin, in order to heal his weakness with the grace of the Sacrament of Reconciliation, is always a ray of hope for the world. (Address, March 9, 2012)

"We never saw anything like this!" The astonished crowd at Capernaum echoes throughout history in the joyous amazement of the Church and the gratitude of each and every believer who discovers, lives, and announces the inexhaustible font of salvation in the Paschal Mystery.

2. An Event both Ecclesial and Personal

The encounter between Jesus and the paralytic of Capernaum takes place in a unique way. Without detailing who takes the initiative, Mark tells us that "they came, bringing to him a paralytic carried by four men" (2:3). Who are the four bearing the stretcher? The parallel texts of Matthew and Luke ignore such details ("And behold, they brought to him a paralytic, lying on his bed," Mt 9:2; "And behold, men were bringing on a bed a man who was paralyzed, Lk 5:18"). Blocked from reaching Jesus by the crowd milling in front of the house, they take a decisive initiative. They make an opening in the roof "above him" (v. 4), and lower the stretcher that carries the paralytic. Jesus "saw their faith," but surprisingly does not speak words of healing to the paralytic. Instead, "Child, your sins are forgiven" (v. 5).

This curious episode highlights the desire and the strong determination of those who want to help the paralytic by bringing him to Jesus. No obstacle can stop them, neither the sick man's problematic condition, nor the road blocked by the crowd, nor the walls of the house that separate them from Jesus. It is in consideration of "their" faith that Jesus proclaims the forgiveness of the paralytic's sins. Exegetes have often identified the four stretcher-bearers with the four disciples whose calling is described shortly before along the banks of the Sea of Galilee (see Mk 1:16-20): "Follow me and I will make you become fishers of men." Jesus' imperative and promise to them seems to begin to take effect in the behavior of the four bearing the stretcher. They go in search of those without access to Jesus, or those who cannot blend in with the crowd because of their illness. To be fishermen means to draw a catch from the sea, to be fishers of men means to snatch men from the brink of death (a condition that the defenseless paralytic represents) in order to safeguard their lives, as the paralytic's first reaction to his healing suggests: "he rose" (v. 12, *ēgerthē*). The same verb is used to describe Jesus' resurrection (Mk 16:6). The task given to the disciples and the action of the stretcher-bearers are joined together, showing that Jesus' paschal mystery is realized and extends out thanks also to their collaboration.

Another detail, also typical of Mark, is worth noting: the stress the text places on the stretcher-bearers' goal. According to Luke, the stretcher is lowered down "before Jesus" (Lk 5:19). Matthew avoids any precise details (see Mt 9:1-8). Mark instead highlights the fact that the point where they make an opening is above where Jesus was. They lower the stretcher on which the paralytic lay (v. 4). The double space connotation makes the two figures — Jesus and the paralytic — coincide in a type of overlay. The two are present in the same point. The place of the illness is the same place where

Jesus is "preaching the word" (v. 2). Where sin is present is the place where the Word saves by forgiving. The place of sin becomes the place of salvation!

The Faith of the Four Stretcher-Bearers

There is a close relationship between the four stretcher-bearers and the forgiveness of sins. It is thanks to "their" faith that Jesus ratifies the pardon of the paralytic. In contrast to the crowd, these men are not merely spectators to Christ's actions. In some way it seems that they are the ones to have provoked the reaction. An ancient interpretation from the baptismal liturgy associates them with the godparents who accompany the catechumen. It is not difficult, however, to see in them a broader reference to the entire Christian community and the task that it performs in God's forgiveness of sins. Everything those four organize and execute has one goal, which they pursue with irrepressible tenacity — to "bring" someone to Jesus. Such lucidity and persistence are connected to the determination with which Jesus carries out the will of God for the Son of man, even to the supreme sacrifice of the Cross, the source of all Christian forgiveness (see Mk 8:31; 9:31; 10:33-34).

The action of the four is thus aligned with the action of Jesus. Forgiveness reaches the paralytic through Jesus' words, words that resound in a context prepared by the four and in which they play a fundamental role. In the account we are not told that the paralytic has faith but that he is transported by the faith of the four! The faith of the believing community opens a space wherein the sinner is reached by God's forgiveness through the encounter with Jesus. It is a fundamental "sacramental" dimension of faith. The forgiveness of sins takes place within an event of the Church.

The Church's mission is here summed up in the formula "to bring someone to Jesus," which, however, does not mean to lead someone "before" Jesus. The four do not simply remove the obstacles on the sinner's path toward Jesus. Rather, the paralytic is lowered down exactly onto the spot where Jesus is, thus allowing a unique and surprising personal encounter with him to take place. More than an act of rescue and compassion, it is a mission of initiation, which participates in the dynamics with which God grants forgiveness and, at the same time, introduces him into the mystery of the power that Jesus manifests in his word and person. It thus appears so clear that salvation comes completely from God but reaches the sinner by uniting him with the mission of Christ and the disciples themselves.

The first thing about the sacrament of confession that the *Catechism of the Catholic Church* highlights is the ecclesial dimension of the apostles' ministry: "In imparting to his apostles his own power to forgive sins the Lord also gives them the authority to reconcile sinners with the Church" (1444) and the consequent task of "moderator of the penitential discipline" (1462) proper to the bishop. The view then broadens when it speaks of the effects of the sacrament:

> This sacrament *reconciles us with the Church*. Sin damages or even breaks fraternal communion. The sacrament of Penance repairs or restores it. In this sense it does not simply heal the one restored to ecclesial communion, but has also a revitalizing effect on the life of the Church which suffered from the sin of one of her members. (*Catechism*, 1469).

The episode of the paralytic of Capernaum, however, delineates a theological perspective in which the ecclesial dimension of this sacrament is even broader and stronger. It extends not only to the moment of the personal celebration of the sacrament before a minister, nor is it limited to the fact that reconciliation with God leads also to reconciliation with the Church. The ecclesial dimension is also prior to, and has, as it were, a performative connotation. It is inherent to the entire penitential path, from the beginning to the end. Here God grants pardon to the sinner because, through the eyes of Jesus, he recognizes the faith that the Church returns to him. It is a threefold perspective of mercy, which in a unique way places God, Jesus, and the Church in relationship.

A certain analogy emerges in the great hymn of Ephesians 1:3–14, where the author declares that redemption, as forgiveness of sins, came forth through the blood of Christ poured out (see v. 7). Such an event of grace takes place on the level of love as fruit of the free will of the Father who, seeing us in Christ and always joined to him, chose us from the foundation of the world, granting us the status of adopted children (v. 3). Reconciliation thus happens within a vision in which the Father "sees" the Church, whose real identity and real foundation lie in being related to Christ.

This theological perspective, at once Trinitarian and ecclesial, is so concentrated in communion that the practice of penance and of pastoral care have likely not yet developed all of its implications and consequences. The liturgy, however, in its educational wisdom, impedes us from forgetting. In the Communion rites of the Eucharistic celebration, at the moment in which the peace promised by Christ is invoked, the priest exclaims, "Look not on our sins, but on the faith of your Church." We are thus brought back each time to that day at Capernaum, to the moment when Christ's eyes rest on the faith of the four stretcher-bearers.

Rise and Go Home

Only at the end of the account in Mark's Gospel does the paralytic take on an active role. In perfect correlation with Jesus' words, "rise, take up your pallet and go home" (2:11), "he rose, and immediately took up the pallet and went out" (v. 12). The immediate and perfect harmony between the command and its execution has, first and foremost, the aim of highlighting the power and effectiveness of Jesus' words. The dispute with the scribes, in fact, focused on the quality of Jesus' "speaking": "Which is easier, to *say* to the paralytic, 'Your sins are forgiven,' or to *say*, 'Rise, take up your pallet and walk'?" (v. 9). The double "saying" highlights everything that is at stake — are Jesus' words true or empty, powerful or illusory? The fact that the paralytic rises forces the doctors of the Law to reexamine their judgments against Jesus.

Prior to this moment, although present throughout the scene, the figure of the paralytic plays an extremely marginal role. Other than his condition as a sick man, we are not given any characteristics. He has no name, nor is he marked by any religious affiliation (pagan, Judean, Pharisee, Levite). Social markers are missing (rich or poor). He neither speaks nor reveals his thoughts, emotions, or reactions. There is an impenetrable wall with one crack that allows us to glimpse his moral condition inherent in Jesus' declaration that his sins are forgiven — he is a sinner. Jesus sees the faith of the four but also knows this man's intimate situation, just as the Pharisees' and scribes' judgment do not escape him, even if they are only in their thoughts (see v. 8). Only Jesus knows the depths, and lays bare the heart, of each person, thereby revealing himself as the prophetic Messiah and Redeemer.

Attention on the paralytic instead comes from another element. In speaking of him, Mark's Gospel twice refers to bringing or carrying. "And they came, bringing to him a paralytic carried by four men" (v. 3). The figure of the sick man is not only impenetrable, but completely defenseless, a description that is in sharp contrast with the chaotic scene of the milling crowd and the stretcher-bearers' ingenuity. It is this inanimate figure, deprived of all willpower and vitality, belonging more to the world of the dead than of the living, whom Jesus, like a father, calls "child." He forgives the sins of this child in the very moment that he reveals himself, guaranteeing that there is no obstacle between him and God. He sees himself declared a "sinner," yet through the same word he rediscovers his vocation as a "child."

The distance that is bridged between the paralytic and Jesus corresponds to the overcoming of the distance that separates God from the sinner. The paralytic thus experiences that by approaching Jesus he comes close to the kingdom of God, where faith, conversion, and good news merge (see Mk 1:15). At the same time, by speaking them aloud, Jesus' words make it clear to everyone that illness and sin are not insurmountable forces that can keep the paralytic ever in their power. God has always considered him to be a "child," never forsaking him, no matter what he may have done. In the encounter with Jesus, the forgiveness of sins is thus joined to the revelation of the sinner's salvation. His original relationship to God, that of a "child," comes back into focus. No one saw it any longer, but Jesus' words that caused him to rise guaranteed that it was never lost or withdrawn.

The power of Jesus' words is manifested in the effect they produce. The paralytic is finally cured, and he reacts with a threefold transformation. He who was lying down arises. He who was carried takes up his pallet. He who could not enter the house returns under his own power. The actions' immediacy amplifies their vitality. The one "carried" finally walks, and the note about the pallet that he takes up as he walks away, though not needing it, suggests that its task was not complete. It may serve to help the paralytic himself bring other sick sinners to Jesus. Thus the circle is closed. The one "carried" is transformed into "the carrier." The one who was lowered down in the shadow of death now walks for all to see. He who was the object of the mercy of God and of the stretcher-bearers now becomes a stretcher-bearer, a "fisher of men," so that others brought to Christ can experience the mysterious encounter of faith, love, and forgiveness, like he did.

CHAPTER TWO

A Father and Two Sons

Just as the dynamics of mercy bring about within us the forgiveness of sins, they are manifested in the parable of the father and the two sons (see Lk 15:11-32), the longest parable of Luke's Gospel and the third in a succession of parables centered on God's behavior and his joy at recovering what was lost (a sheep, Lk 15:1-7; a coin, Lk 15:8-10; a son, Lk 15:11-32). Like the description of the paralytic at Capernaum, the characters in Luke's parable are described in a nearly anonymous way. The only interest of the account is in the difficult relations between the father and his two sons centered on the issues of fatherhood, filial relations, and fraternal bonds. Forgiveness and mercy are first and foremost personal realities, events that penetrate man in his innermost depths and reciprocal relations, upsetting life in an unexpected and almost miraculous way. In the account it is therefore necessary to pay particular attention to the characters' actions and words. Here their true feelings, their most deeply held values, and their real aims emerge. And an unexpected picture forms — a unique fatherhood, disconcerting filial relationships, and a brotherhood to put back together.

1. A Son's Return

From the beginning of the parable, the figure of the younger son presents two obscure and worrisome points. He is introduced into the scene without any preliminaries, asking the father for his share of the property. He does not explain the reasons for such a request, nor does the father require them. The fact that he simply asks for what "falls to me" (v. 12) shows that he is not claiming anything undue. He is aware of his status as a son, and yet his wish is to leave and go far away. The inheritance is meant to be divided, but the elder son is not mentioned in the account. In abandoning the home in which he intends to leave nothing behind (he "gathered *all* he had"), he radically breaks the tie that binds him to his father and brother, yet that does not seem to be very important to him, intent as he is on carrying out his own plan.

The sudden way that "not many days later, the younger son gathered all he had and took his journey into a far country, and there he squandered his property in loose living" (v. 13) illuminates the true motivations underlying his request to the father. Hasty as it was, the son's wish is the fruit of a free and conscious decision. He will have no one to blame if he finds himself in the dramatic condition of risking starvation. It is his fault, and the responsibility is entirely personal. But his words communicate more than they say vis-à-vis his father and elder brother. As a son his claims on his inheritance are legitimate, and his father poses no objection. Nor do we hear any recrimination from the elder brother. And yet the fact the he asks for what "falls to me" implies a patrimonial division of the inheritance. The claim is thus directed to the father, but as if he were already dead! The fact that he rushes to prepare his departure for a far country shows that the distance is no longer just geographic. Whatever the motives for his departure, for the youngest son the wish for autonomy counts more than his sonship. In his sudden departure, the emphasis on the separation shows that the figures of the father and of the brother are already dead in the life project the youngest son pursues.

He goes far from his father, far from his elder brother, for a dissolute life of pleasure. All too often this detail has driven preaching focused on moral stigmas. Yet the account aims rather at highlighting the story's unforeseen wrinkle. From the very beginning the young man experiences that the faraway life he desired at all costs turns out to be a tragic choice in which he loses all of his dignity. He was seeking his own autonomy far from his father and a clean break from home, but he finds himself having to serve by feeding swine, a humiliating job for a Jew, which furthermore does not even feed him. The "far country" loses all attractiveness and displays two characteristics. It does not make him wealthy — it causes him to spend everything he has — and it empties him from within. In addition, it is a place of famine, which can provide no nourishment whatsoever. For the young son the future holds only hopeless exhaustion. And yet this catastrophe leads to a new discovery, the way in which the father welcomes him. And the father's decision will in turn provoke an unexpected reaction in the elder son. This plotline of sin and mercy, guilt and forgiveness, moves from surprise to surprise.

The Experience of Sin

The parable does not give a definition of sin nor does it focus particularly on the motivations that cause the younger son to leave home. Everything instead aims at preparing the justification for his return to the father. This silence regarding the reasons behind the bad choices pushes us to question ourselves about the origin of the evil within each of us and about why man continues to seek a country far from his father. It is a silence that leaves space for a thousand answers (selfishness, envy, loss of reference points, false values, indifference to one's neighbor, etc.). Confessors and penitents could easily make their own additions, shedding light on individual, social, and ecclesial motivations that underlie the evils of our time. But the evidence simply shows that sin is something innate to us, to the point that its repetition lulls the conscience to sleep. In order to realize this, it would be enough to do the exercise of trying to recall our first sin in order to recognize the impossibility of formulating an answer. In simple terms, as far as we are aware, we must recognize that sin has always been with us, ever present in its diverse aspects of greater or lesser gravity.

Upon this presence, as mysterious as it is unsettling, the text of Genesis 3 has meditated, speaking of the tempting serpent, "more subtle than any other wild creature that the LORD God had made" (v. 1). Adam and Eve are in the Garden of Eden, literally, the "garden of delights," and the serpent is presented as alien. He does not belong to the garden but is a creature of the wild, yet he suddenly appears where the man and the woman are. Some Fathers of the Church wondered how this beast could have entered the garden, who and when it was introduced. It is the same question that the servants ask in the parable of the sower, "Sir, did you not sow good seed in your field? How then has it weeds?" (Mt 13:27). It is the same question that is repeated every time sin and its evil and sorrowful consequences provoke scandal before our eyes.

The Bible avoids any philosophical explanation. Evil is presented but not explained. It simply "was." In the moment Adam and Eve began their human adventure, the serpent nestled into their intimacy and was present to their thoughts, words, and actions. He is persuasive, able to suggest "far countries" beyond any obligation or limit ("you will be like God," Gn 3:5), and above all able to distort and deform the vision of God and the relationship with him. Like the younger son in the parable, Adam and Eve find themselves emptied and miserable, unable even to look at each other. Their nakedness is now the mirror of the truth of their guilt, a view they cannot bear.

So what is sin? Luke's parable suggests the image of "separation" from the Father. Sin is everything that distances us from him and our brethren and comes to upset our hearts. Sin is whatever does not let us live a full life. Sin is everything that keeps us from recognizing the Father's house as ours, causing us to forget that we are brothers and sisters. Finally, sin is everything that degrades our filial relationship and our fraternal relationship.

Thus in approaching the Sacrament of Reconciliation to receive God's forgiveness, it is important that the Christian have a mature certainty and avoid danger. An authentic faith life keeps the conscience vigilant. The disciple who follows the Lord knows that the journey is in truth and is not afraid therefore to lay bare his heart before the Father who can make it "new" (see Ez 11:19). "Through such an admission man looks squarely at the sins he is guilty of, takes responsibility for them, and thereby opens himself again to God and to the communion of the Church in order to make a new future possible" (*Catechism*, 1455).

On the other hand, in identifying one's own sins, he avoids letting himself be carried away by the somewhat petty calculation that tends to speculate about God's love: "How far can I push this behavior with impunity? I can, but within what limits? If I don't cross this line, is it okay?" It is a cheap mindset that puts forth the minimum necessary in the relationship with the Father. Such a perspective generally reduces our ethical life, our witness of faith, and our ascribing to the Church an infinite set of rules that "unfortunately" have to be respected and make the celebration of the Sacrament of Reconciliation ever more painful to the penitent — and to the confessor as well! It frustrates the spiritual life and leads the believer to be closed to the plan that God has for him in entrusting himself to God's inexhaustible mercy, and instead snuffs out the enthusiasm for the Faith. It obscures its beauty by inexorably weakening the dynamics of the Christian life. As Pope Francis reminded us, "The problem is not that we are sinners, but that we do not allow ourselves to be transformed by the encounter with Christ in love" (Homily, May 17, 2013).

So we miss the target and are not able to achieve the main goal. What is that? To live as sons and daughters. It is the Crucified and Risen One, the blessed Son, who shows us how an authentic filial relationship evolves. It is a journey of freedom — an exodus from oneself with no return, a freedom made for loving the Father and others to the point of abandonment on the cross. It is this same freedom that he asks of his disciples in order to receive the gift of the life of God.

The Experience of Forgiveness

The younger brother's monologue begins with an observation. In his father's house the hired servants have food in abundance, "but I perish here with hunger!" (Lk 15:17). It is hunger, not remorse at having caused his father pain, that leads him to go home. That "return within" is not a sign of conversion, as many think. Instead he now realizes the reality into which he has sunk, gripped by a fundamental need that he cannot satisfy. He is starving to death. His survival instinct is what reminds him of home. It is the desire for good food that moves his words, not his relationship with his father. It is a calculation of interest, rather than a sincere repentance. And indeed, even though he confesses, "Father, I have sinned against heaven and before you; I am no longer worthy to be called your son" (vv. 18-19), the young man proposes as a punishment exactly what his plan suggests, "treat me as one of your hired servants," a condition that is a good deal better than feeding swine.

There is another clue that causes suspicion about the young man's true intentions. The monologue acts as a preparatory speech, but once he has reached his father, the son omits the initial phrase — he does not say that it was hunger that made him return! He is sly and does not mention the real reason. Once his strategy for obtaining forgiveness is set, he begins to carry out the plan. "And he arose and came to his father" (v. 20). It is impossible not to be perplexed by such behavior that manipulates the father's feelings and relationship behind the cover of a religiously tinged discourse. The calculation is undeniable and the confession is very self-serving.

The younger son's sneakiness brings out the image he has of his father, that of a severe and just judge who can be tamed with nice words. The plan that he devised begins to crumble, however, precisely because of his father's unexpected actions. "But while he was yet at a distance, his father saw him and had compassion, and ran and embraced him and kissed him" (v. 20). The urgency of his father's movements proves that his embrace does not depend on his son's excuses. In fact, the father is not waiting for his son to speak!

This way of acting therefore, does not depend on nor is it commensurate with the son's words. At this point the young man can say anything, but he has no need to lie or to hide the reasons for his return. He has nothing to fear, his father has run to meet him, has embraced him, and has kissed him, in an unmistakable attitude that puts an end to any subtle strategy.

The father has no reproach for his son — "Oh, how you made me suffer, but I am happy to have you back!" or "Have you finally figured out how wrong you were?" For the father, the only thing that matters is that his son has returned. Indeed, as soon as the son launches into his speech and declares that he is no longer worthy of being his son, the father interrupts him. For the father, those words are unbearable and inadmissible, a possibility they cannot even be considered. Thus the son discovers that in his father's heart he has always had a home and that he never ceased to be a son. No wrong choice, no reproachable behavior, no pain he caused have ever made him less of a son for his father. The calculating son now sees a face of his father that he never expected and which he discovered only by returning home. He is neither a naive nor severe judge, but one who loves without calculations and without measure. The words that the young man directs to his father after being embraced and kissed can now burst forth from his heart without fear, "Father, I have sinned against heaven and before you." Within this reborn relationship the father's gifts to his son only amplify his love, which has never lessened, and reestablish the signs of filial dignity the son thought he had lost. Just like Jesus with the paralytic of Capernaum ("Child, your sins are forgiven," Mk 2:5), this father also gives back to his son his true identity.

2. Entering the Father's House?

In the second part of the parable, the elder son enters the scene. The note that he "was in the field" (v. 25) is curious, because it is the same place the younger son was before returning to his father, "So he went and joined himself to one of the citizens of that country, who sent him into his fields to feed swine" (v. 15). The younger son ventured into a far country whereas the elder son never went far from home. The former gives himself over to a dissolute life, squandering his goods, while the latter occupies himself with a life of work. Nevertheless, as different and contrary as their lives have been, both brothers are led to the same point: they are *in the fields*, and it is from the fields that they return to their father's house.

A number of biblical texts use the image of the field in a negative sense. It is the dwelling place of the tempting serpent and of wild animals (see Gn 3:1), a place of death (Cain raises his hand against his brother Abel in the fields [Gn 4:8]), a place of violence (the Hebrew slaves are forced to labor in the fields [Ex 1:14]), a threatening prophetic image (Hos 2:14; Jer 26:18), and a place of struggle (Mt 13:24-30). Throughout the parable, in fact, the two brothers show no signs of brotherhood. The younger never mentions the elder, who in turn refuses to recognize him ("But when this son of *yours* came," Lk 15:30). In the end, however, both brothers share more than they realize. They are both far from the father and from his wish to see them as "brothers." He, instead, calls both of them with the title of "son" (vv. 24, 31) and invites each to enter the house, so as to participate in the feast where the father returns each to the other as "your brother" (v. 32).

There are other features that seem to unite the two brothers. Apparently, if the eldest son works hard in the fields, it means that in the father's house being a son is not an acceptable reason for doing nothing and living a life of leisure. Was it perhaps for this reason that the youngest son decided to go away? But despite the different choices, one for dissolute living and the other for working, when they refer to their lives with their father, both characterize it as that of an employee. In fact, they share the same criteria based on the logic of retribution: I have sinned therefore I deserve the punishment of no longer being your son; I have always served you so I deserve recompense from you. The younger one does not dare ask for more, while the elder makes it an object of reproach to his father, "Behold, these many years I have served you, and I never disobeyed your command; yet you never gave me a kid, that I might make merry with my friends" (v. 29).

From opposing sides, there emerges the same calculating look that prejudices both brothers from experiencing the father's infinitely generous heart. And it is he who stands again as a mighty figure, an absolutely exceptional fatherhood, who welcomes the younger son unconditionally and shows the elder son that he does not need to ask for anything because "you are always with me, and all that is mine is yours" (v. 31). Toward his children, therefore, he does not and has never calculated anything — he simply always intended to share everything. His fatherhood is pure relatedness toward them, bursting forth with tenderness and love without measure.

The Mentality of a Hired Servant

Upon hearing music and dances, why does the eldest son not enter the house but instead calls a servant to receive information? Being so close to his father for such a long time, does he already suspect something? Had his father already announced his intentions in the event of the return of his brother? Is his indignation aimed at getting his father to change his mind? These are all possible answers. The text, however, aims to highlight the contrast between the words of the servant, which invite him to recognize his family ties (*"Your brother* has come, and *your father* has killed the fatted calf," v. 27), and those that the son instead directs to his father ("But when this *son of yours* came, who has devoured *your living* with harlots, you killed *for him* the fatted calf!" v. 30). He denies a bond with his brother and mocks his father's behavior, distancing himself from both. He does not want to enter the house of his father because by now his heart lives in "a far country."

In comparison with the younger brother, he emphasizes his long and excellent service and loyalty to his father's commands. Its presentation is a sort of exemplary résumé, but his relation with his father is described very coldly, in terms of "obedience" and "commands." He obeyed his laws, so he expected recompense from him, although not in keeping with his toils: at least one kid "to make merry with my friends" (v. 29). Yet his father and brother are not invited to the party that he envisions! Would he ever be able to accept the invitation to join the party that his father has prepared for the younger son?

Accepting the Invitation

A difficulty emerges. Why did the father not immediately invite the eldest son, and why did he start the festivities without him? Why did he not send for him or wait for him to return from the fields? The parable does not offer an answer but leaves it clear that if the party starts, it is solely the father's indisputable decision ("let us eat and make merry," v. 23). It does not depend on the son's wishes but stems directly from "compassion" (v. 20) and the abounding joy of the father at his son who "is alive again" (v. 24), and it cannot be put on hold. For the father's heart there is no alternative: "It was fitting to make merry and be glad" (v. 32). The oldest son can now only decide whether to join in the festivities and share his father's feelings and values, or refuse and rebel. The open ending of the parable does not say what the eldest son's answer is. Both scenes, the one of the younger son (vv. 12-24) and that of the eldest son (vv. 25-32), end with the words of their father. They determine the course of the story and question every reader who, together with the two sons, is given a share of the father's heart. It is necessary to compare oneself to his viewpoint, his reasons and his choices, which are the only values at stake. At the end of the parable, in fact, everyone is placed before a choice — either enter the house and join the party or stay away without tasting the father's joy, refusing his merciful embrace, and without wanting to accept his forgiveness that restores life and makes us brothers.

3. A Father's Compassion

While at the beginning of the parable the figure of the father appears to be a rather minor one, it gains consistency from the moment his younger son is in sight of the house and eventually fulfills the role of the protagonist, determining the direction of the whole story. What moves the father is clear from the beginning. At the sight of his son still far away, the father "had compassion" (v. 20). It is this profound pity that produces the rapid succession of his actions. He runs to meet his son, embraces him, and kisses him. The verb (which translates the Hebrew *rakhamim*) emphasizes an almost visceral compassion. He cannot wait until the child arrives at home, and rushes to him, moved by this unstoppable force. The prophets in particular described this disturbing emotion in God: "Look down from heaven and see, / from your holy and glorious habitation. / Where are your zeal and your might? / The yearning of your heart and your compassion / are withheld from me" (Is 63:15; see also Is 49:15; Zech 1:16; Ps 145:9). Compassion is described as the exact opposite of impassiveness or hardness of heart, and is the fundamental quality of the God who is mercy, tenderness to the point of physical emotion, a zeal and passion that always lead him to effective action.

Even the conversation that the father has with his youngest son shows the depth of the mystery of his mercy. With great tenderness he ignores the word "sin" that the son has just uttered, and he does not dwell on the ambiguous motives that led him home. The only thing he thinks of is his son's narrow escape from danger. Death was depriving him of his son! For the father, the only thing that counts is that his son is now there, back home, his child's life ransomed by a love that never wavered.

The father calls his son's distancing (and the consequent separation from his father and brother) death, and his return equivalent to a return to life (see v. 24). His return to this life was a long journey with the typical Easter connotations. In his passage from death to life the younger son is mysteriously associated with the paschal mystery of Christ crucified and risen. Conversion as a return to the father is the dynamic of the Christian life, a tension supported by a love that transcends imagination and which reflects the event that Love manifests beyond measure, the Lord's Passover. The life of the Christian, therefore, can only be a life that is consummately Paschal.

The Gifts of Mercy

Out of the father's exceptional joy spring the gifts the son receives. In them various meanings can be drawn from the vast symbolic heritage of the Christian tradition.

The best robe is immediately associated with the new state of life into which the father reintegrates his son and suggests typically baptismal imagery, "For as many of you as were baptized into Christ have put on Christ" (Gal 3:27). As a result: "But now put them all away: anger, wrath, malice, slander, and foul talk from your mouth. Do not lie to one another, seeing that you have put off the old man with his practices and have put on the new man, who is being renewed in knowledge after the image of his creator" (Col 3:8-10). Through baptism the Christian life is here defined in new terms, with a behavior unthinkable for anyone who remains immersed in the heaviness of sin. In fact, if the one baptized is "born again" his new life can only be the life *of* Christ and life *in* Christ. The Letter to the Colossians stresses that this growth happens through a continuous renewal. In this way, the Sacrament of Reconciliation is profoundly linked with the Sacrament of Baptism:

> Nevertheless the new life received in Christian initiation has not abolished the frailty and weakness of human nature, nor the inclination to sin that tradition calls *concupiscence,* which remains in the baptized such that with the help of the grace of Christ they may prove themselves in the struggle of Christian life.

> Christ's call to conversion continues to resound in the lives of Christians. This *second conversion* is an uninterrupted task for the whole Church.... It is the movement

of a "contrite heart," drawn and moved by grace to respond to the merciful love of God who loved us first. (*Catechism*, 1426,1428).

The *ring on his hand* indicates the power that is restored to the son. To grant full powers to Joseph, son of Jacob, Pharaoh gives him his ring (see Gn 41:42), as does the Persian king Ahasuerus toward his confidant Haman (Est 3:10). The ring is a symbol of the bond and union. The son is restored to full communion with the Father and partakes of his lordship.

Shoes on his feet. Wearing shoes and sandals was a privilege of free men. Prisoners of war and slaves had to walk barefoot (see Is 20:2,4). The son is thus reinstated in his ancient rights.

The last indication of joy given by the father regards preparations for a party. The order to prepare the fatted calf and the explicit command to eat is an allusion to the feast of fat things that seals the covenant between God and humanity. "On this mountain the LORD of hosts will make for all peoples a feast of fat things, a feast of choice wines — of fat things full of marrow, of choice wines well refined" (Is 25:6). In particular, the Book of Deuteronomy ties the theme of the banquet to that of joyous celebration in the presence of Yahweh:

> You shall not do so to the LORD your God. But you shall seek the place which the LORD your God will choose out of all your tribes to put his name and make his habitation there; there you shall go, and there you shall bring your burnt offerings and your sacrifices, your tithes and the offering that you present, your votive offerings, your freewill offerings, and the firstlings of your herd and of your flock; and there you shall eat before the LORD your God, and you shall rejoice, you and your households, in all that you undertake, in which the LORD your God has blessed you (Dt 12:4-7; see also Dt 14:22-24; 16:10-17).

In the New Testament there are many texts that refer to participation in a joyful family feast. In the Gospel of Luke, the parable of
the guests invited to a grand dinner foreshadows the three parables
on mercy (see 14:16-24). In the final scene, the banquet the father
is to prepare for his returned son has a ritual and ceremonial value.
Its purpose is to celebrate the one who has taken a step, marking
his transformation. It also celebrates the mutual solidarity that now
links father to son, the bond between them — their unity.

Many have taken this as a reference to the Passover meal that
Christ celebrated at the Last Supper, in which the covenant between
God and man is established forever in his blood (see Lk 22:20). The
explicit invitation to participate in his banquet is taken by the angel
in the Revelation to John, enjoining this command: "Write this:
Blessed are those who are invited to the marriage supper of the
Lamb" (19:9). It is the blessedness that, with some adaptation, is
included in the liturgy in the invitation to Eucharistic communion.

After baptism, the Eucharist is also connected to the Sacrament of Reconciliation. It reveals to the Christian community the
need for ongoing conversion and provides the reconciling power
of the Lord's Passover: "Daily conversion and penance find their
source and nourishment in the Eucharist, for in it is made present
the sacrifice of Christ which has reconciled us with God. Through
the Eucharist those who live from the life of Christ are fed and
strengthened" (*Catechism*, 1436).

The Feast of Forgiveness

The father tells his eldest son "it was fitting to make merry" (v.
32). The father obeys a superior logic that he has no choice but to
follow, a logic that is both different and higher than the eldest son's
way of seeing: "He loves; he doesn't know how to do anything else!"
(Pope Francis, Homily, March 28, 2014). His fatherhood places the
relationship to his child before all else — this is the meaning of his
being father. If his son "was dead," he would cease to be his father!
By returning to his father, he "is alive," has returned to the life of a

son, thus reviving the father himself who immediately runs to meet him. The eldest son is called to realize the circularity of this deep love that binds the father to the son, a circularity that applies also to him. By finding the son, the father can give him back his brother, without which even the eldest son would have lost his own identity as brother. So the deep compassion that drives the father's action finds its greatest joy in seeing the sons gathered as brothers. Fatherhood then reaches its height and shines in all its light.

Pope Benedict XVI gave the following summary of the parable of the prodigal son:

> This passage of St Luke constitutes one of the peaks of spirituality and literature of all time. Indeed, what would our culture, art and more generally our civilization be without this revelation of a God the Father so full of mercy? It never fails to move us and every time we hear or read it, it can suggest to us ever new meanings. Above all, this Gospel text has the power of speaking to us of God, of enabling us to know his Face and, better still, his Heart. After Jesus has told us of the merciful Father, things are no longer as they were before. We now know God; he is our Father who out of love created us to be free and endowed us with a conscience, who suffers when we get lost and rejoices when we return. For this reason, our relationship with him is built up through events, just as it happens for every child with his parents: at first he depends on them, then he asserts his autonomy; and, in the end if he develops well he reaches a mature relationship based on gratitude and authentic love. (Angelus, March 14, 2010)

In illustrating this wise pedagogy of God's mercy, the parable of the father and the two sons is not intended to make us meditate on the abstract mystery of love that forgives, but urges every person to have recourse to that mercy in the name of Christ and in union with him. We are thus transported by the Love that saves to recognize our infidelities and confess our sins. Thus, by revealing the love of God, the Word of the Lord continues to become flesh in the life of every believer, and impresses upon his wounded conscience the face of the Father who is rich in compassion. The Church therefore has no choice but to profess God's mercy in the truth that Revelation hands down to us, and gives witness to it by putting herself at its service:

> In the light of this inexhaustible parable of the mercy that wipes out sin, the Church takes up the appeal that the parable contains and grasps her mission of working, in imitation of the Lord, for the conversion of hearts and for the reconciliation of people with God and with one another — these being two realities that are intimately connected. (St. John Paul II, *Reconciliatio et Paenitentia*, 6)

CHAPTER THREE

Of Debts and Debtors

In the Sermon on the Mount, the first and the largest among the discourses of Jesus in the Gospel according to Matthew (Chapters 5-7), the central passage focuses on the three classical forms of Jewish piety: almsgiving, prayer, and fasting (see 6:1-18). In the heart of his teaching on prayer, and thus at the absolute center of the whole discourse, is the Lord's Prayer (6:9-13). The centrality given to the prayer taught by Jesus to his disciples and to the crowd shows that it is a priceless gift, a precious stone set within his teaching. The relationship of the Christian with the Father, in fact, is the basis of his whole being and all his actions.

The prayer consists of seven requests (seven is the number of totality and perfection). The first three relate primarily to God's initiative, highlighted by possessive adjectives making reference in the second person (*Thy* name, *Thy* kingdom, *Thy* will, vv. 9-10); the last four are requests pertaining to fundamental human needs, formulated using possessives in the first person (give *us our* daily bread, forgive *us our* debts, lead *us* not, but deliver *us*). Notice that the fifth request takes the form of a petition for forgiveness.

Speaking of "debts" (in Greek *opheilémata*) and "debtors" (*opheilétais*, Mt 6:12, NABRE), Matthew uses legal-commercial language. Debts, in fact, indicate primarily those that were to be paid back in cash to avoid an additional penalty. To compensate for the resulting social imbalances, the law of the Sabbatical ordered freeing of slaves, precisely those persons who had become slaves because they could not pay their debts (see Ex 21:2-6; Dt 15:1-11). In a parallel way, the Gospel of Luke uses the expression "forgive us our sins" (in Greek *amartías*, 11:4), intending to theologically clarify the request — debts to God are "sins." The two versions thus converge, and in reciting the Our Father, the Christian uses the term "trespasses." We should not, however, forget the primary value of the term used by Matthew, because it is a reminder of the parable of the good king and the unforgiving servant (Mt 18:21-35), a parable found only in Matthew and in which he uses the term "debts" (*opheilémata*) for the second and last time. From this parable we can understand the request contained in the Our Father to forgive our debts.

1. The Parable of the Good King and the Unforgiving Servant

The parable starts with a dialogue between Peter and Jesus on reconciliation among the disciples: "Lord, how often shall my brother sin against me, and I forgive him? As many as seven times?" (Mt 18:21). The question seems to imply a practice of reconciliation within the Christian community, about which certain criteria needed to be clarified. Peter's starting offer is certainly generous: "As many as seven times?" Jesus' response is surprising, though. We must not make calculations. The disciple must adopt a style according to the dynamics of the kingdom of heaven, in which mercy is boundless and produces forgiveness without measure and without reservation.

The dizzying perspective opened up by Jesus is illustrated by the parable, in which the main effect comes from a huge and un-payable debt accumulated by a servant to his lord. Three scenes follow, of which the first two are symmetrical but contrary. First, he describes the action of the king who forgives (see vv. 23-27), then that of the servant who punishes (vv. 28-30), and the third compares the two modes of action (vv. 31-34), culminating in the last words that the king pronounces: "Should not you have had mercy on your fellow servant, as I had mercy on you?" (v. 33). The contrast is amplified by some differences: the gap in social status between king and servant in the first scene and the parity between servant and fellow servant (*doulos* and *syndoūlos*) in the second, the huge debt in the first and the insignificant one in the second, and the roles played by the first servant — insolvent debtor and then ruthless creditor. The aim is to awaken the idea of the immeasurable vastness of God's forgiveness, especially when compared to the limited and somewhat petty human reality.

A Crippling Debt

At first the master obliges the servant to pay his debt, ten thousand talents, a huge sum if you consider that the total annual income of Herod's kingdom was nine hundred talents, and total tax revenues of Galilee and Perea did not exceed two hundred talents. The story aims to show that in no way could such a debt be honored by a servant whose desperate plea ("he fell on his knees") is as moving as unreal: "Have patience with me, and I will pay you everything" (v. 26). No extension would be sufficient to pay off such a debt! The truth is that he cannot get rid of it in any way. The unexpected solution comes (again!) from "pity" (v. 27) that moves his master to action. The first order to sell him, "with his wife and children and all that he had" (v. 25), to settle the debt, is instead followed by the surprising decision to release him with the debt entirely forgiven.

The forgiveness of a debt so large should result in some attitude of gratitude and compassion from those who benefit, especially if the debtor is a fellow servant — that is, one whose poverty and need he should know well, having experienced it firsthand. And more so, since the debt is very modest when compared to the one just forgiven. But this does not happen. "As he went out" (v. 28), the servant ran into a coworker who in turn owes him a hundred denarii. For a servant, one hundred denarii roughly corresponded to little more than pay for three months of work, a figure not quite immaterial when viewed in terms of commutative justice between colleagues. But the introduction of the parable pushes us to another comparison: "A king who wished to settle accounts with his servants" (v. 23). The axis of evaluation is not horizontal, among peers, but vertical, between a king and a servant. When a king forgives an immense debt to a servant, what should one expect from the servant? A further particular should attract our attention: "When he began the reckoning, one was brought to him who owed him ten thousand talents" (v. 24). The servant's hearing is held at the beginning of the king's judicial activity. We can assume that this activity will be continued. Moreover, we do not know who brought the debtor servant to him. It is definitely their act that forces the servant to settle accounts before the king-judge. In other words, it is not the master who called the servant directly. He calls him to account because others have spoken of him. Once he sees the debt is canceled, the servant should at least have been more careful and aware. The settling of accounts that the king absolves pivots, in fact, on the relations that the "fellow servants" (*syndouloi*) weave amongst themselves.

Settling Accounts

In the second scene, the ruthlessness of the servant creditor toward a coworker is harshly underlined from the beginning: "Seizing him by the throat," he orders him, "Pay what you owe!" (v. 28). The servant does not require anything but what is owed him. It is a question of justice, and none of us would object if he had not just pleaded for his own special treatment. Through the forgiveness of the debt, the servant had not only received a gift of mercy, but had also been introduced into the heart of the master, whose different way of assessing the debt and the debtor had been coveted by him. In his heart, justice is not simply proportional to the amount owed. By sharing his compassion, the king had shown that mercy was possible and feasible, fulfilling his plea beyond hope. Amazingly, the king wanted to start "settling accounts" with debt relief!

Having become a sharer in the heart of the king, and having experienced his mysterious justice, the servant could and should have extended the same mercy to others. The request for an extension by his debtor coworker (see v. 29) is exactly parallel to what he had asked his master (v. 26), but it does not obtain the desired — and at this point merited — effect. The ruthlessness of the servant is completely unjustifiable! His debtor colleague is thrown in prison "till he should pay the debt" (v. 30).

The Final Judgment

The last act of the parable begins with the reaction of the other "servants" (*syndouloi*) (v. 31). They are "greatly distressed," a combination of pain and sadness. The preposition *syn* (literally, "with") expresses a particular bond between these servants. They form a cohesive group in service to the king-judge. Since they serve, he gives directives to which they must adhere. In other words, the servants are obliged to take on the perspective of the master, that of compassion. It is from that standpoint that they evaluate the act of merciless servant, so "they went and reported to their lord all that had taken place" (v. 31). Unlike the merciless servant, in the "servants" (*syndouloi*) the mercy of the landlord has reformulated their sense of justice. This is to be the rule that governs their relationship and their service. Lacking pity, the merciless servant ignored what the master had actually taught him and distanced himself from his companions. "Then his lord summoned him and said to him, 'You wicked servant!'" (v. 32). A wicked servant cannot be in his service; he is merely "a man" brought before him.

The identity of the Christian community is thus traced out. The Lord's disciples constitute a brotherhood based on mercy that the Lord has poured out upon them, and the forgiveness of debts is its fundamental rule. Unlimited and unconditional forgiveness determines fraternal relations, activating a service inspired by and performed in mercy. So the dynamics of the kingdom of God are realized in the world, Christologically transfiguring "man" into "servant," in the image of the one who, "though he was in the form of God ... emptied himself, taking the form of a servant ... and became obedient unto death, even death on a cross" (Phil 2:6-8).

Not having been carried away by the dynamism of the master's compassionate love, the servant finds himself caught in a dramatic and disastrous epilogue. The master's sentence is based on the concept of justice that the servant adopted toward his companion. The king's declaration, "I forgave you all that debt because you pleaded with me" (v. 32), demonstrates that his servant's request was a prayer that went directly to his heart. A rhetorical question follows, "Should not you have had mercy on your fellow servant, as (Greek ōs kai, comparative value) I had mercy on you?" By entering the mercy of his master, the servant would have had to imitate his heart and have mercy on his coworker, carried away by the overflowing and unconditional compassion that he received. The conclusion is bitter and astounds us as much as the initial mercy: "And in anger his lord delivered him to the jailers [in Greek, torturers], till he should pay all his debt" (v. 34). Ultimately, the master relates to the servant according to the desires he had gradually expressed. His begging moved his master's heart to mercy. In claiming what was owed, he put his own justice into motion, a justice that, in not taking into account the immensity of his debt, becomes his undoing.

The story also highlights that the face of God, compassionate or angry, is reflected in the faces of his servants — compassionate when implementing fraternal forgiveness, angry when mercy has no place. Finally, this parable reveals a dynamic of forgiveness in three stages: first, there is the unmerited and immense forgiveness of the master of his servant. Later, it extends to shape the relations of those who serve the master. Finally, the brotherhood born of and nourished by that forgiveness, in turn, becomes the basis and reference for a final judgment. It is a development that has its origin and its fulfillment in the figure of the king, but the performance of which involves the servants, obliging them to live according to the heart of the one who appears infinitely merciful.

The final words of Jesus respond to the original question of Peter: "So also (Greek *ōs kai*, sequential value) my heavenly Father will do to every one of you, if you do not forgive your brother from your heart" (v. 35). Forgiveness comes from a remission of unpayable debt born out of the heavenly Father's love. This same love also stimulates the heart of the Christian to assume with sincerity and good will the logic of forgiveness between brothers. It is the commitment with which the believing community lives the experience of brotherhood as service.

2. Forgive Us Our Debts

The question of forgiveness of debts contained in the Lord's Prayer should be understood against the background of the teaching of the parable. First a plea, "Forgive us our debts," then a subordinate clause, "as we forgive our debtors." The petition refers to the servant's plea to his master. The subordinate clause evokes how the servant should have behaved with his fellow debtor: with the compassionate behavior of the king toward him. When reciting the Lord's Prayer, the Christian thus takes on the view of the king in the parable. He prays to the "Father in heaven" (Mt 6:9), who is also "Our Father," in tune with his heart and his will. He is a servant (*syndoulos*) in service within a community that has brotherhood as its fulcrum and hallmark.

The fact that forgiveness must be asked for in prayer implies a conscientious (but not fearful!) attitude. Because the debt is huge, the Christian knows that he is an insolvent servant. Is it possible to fully live up to a mercy so great? The community of believers knows its limits and does not hide them. It asks, knowing that it cannot rely on its own strength. It knows that forgiveness and brotherhood are above all the fruit of grace and that they can only be received as a gift from a heart filled with love like that of the Father, a Father "in heaven" and "ours." And since Christ teaches the Lord's Prayer, it is through his words that the believer's plea raises to the Father. Just as it is through him that the compassionate heart of the Father manifested itself beyond measure on the wood of the cross, it is also through him that forgiveness is given and moves the disciples to recognize themselves as brothers: "All this is from God, who through Christ reconciled us to himself and gave us the ministry of reconciliation" (2 Cor 5:18).

3. We Forgive Our Debtors

Many discussions have arisen about how to understand the literary connection the Lord's Prayer establishes between God's forgiveness and forgiveness among brothers. Some doubts arise even among believers when they read, "as we also [Greek ōs kai] have forgiven our debtors." Would Jesus make an act of God depend on human action? Is the love of God commensurate to the ethical commitment of a Christian? Do we receive forgiveness because we are sinners or to the extent that we are not? Is forgiveness a quid pro quo, a kind of barter with God?

The parable of the servant with the huge debt gets rid of such interpretations. The servant receives forgiveness before meeting his fellow debtor, and only later, in the final judgment, does the master ask him to account for how he acted. The Greek expression "like us" (ōs kai) occurs twice in the parable, but each with a different value. In Matthew 18:33, it has comparative value by comparing the forgiveness of the servant with that of the master. Within the meaning of comparative, the request for forgiveness of the Lord's Prayer can be understood in two ways: "forgive us our debts *in the same manner and to the same extent* with which we forgive our debtors." It would not, however, be a quantitative correspondence, but a declaration.

The Christian community shows that it has no prospect but that of forgiveness as extended and taught by Jesus. It tells the Father that it is its own rule of life and therefore is not afraid to ask forgiveness of him. A second interpretation takes the comparative value of the particle as a reference to eschatological forgiveness: Christians, as good "servants" (*syndouloi*), conform to the perspective of God's forgiveness and not that of the merciless servant. They therefore request this be taken into account at the last judgment: "Forgive us our debts, *as we also* forgive [what we are remitting] our debtors." In Matthew 18:35, "so also" (*ōs kai*) instead has a consecutive value. The wrath of the heavenly Father is the consequence of mercy not granted. In this case, the Christian prays that the unmerited forgiveness that he receives from the Father be an abundant and inexhaustible source of forgiveness that he pours onto his brothers: "Forgive us our debts *so that we too* forgive our debtors."

From the literary standpoint it is impossible to determine with certainty which of the two options is preferable. Their comparative value, however, is noted in the verses immediately following the Lord's Prayer: "For if you forgive men their trespasses, your heavenly Father also will forgive you; but if you do not forgive men their trespasses, neither will your Father forgive your trespasses" (Mt 6:14-15). Perhaps it is therefore preferable to give a consecutive meaning to the request for forgiveness first expressed in prayer, so as to maintain both meanings. In this way the dynamism of forgiveness is maintained in three stages: God's forgiveness creates the capacity for forgiveness in believers (see Mt 6:12) and the forgiveness that they offer to others makes way for their forgiveness at God's last judgment (Mt 6:14-15). All this seems borne out by the last two requests formulated in the Lord's Prayer, those concerning temptation and deliverance from evil, a kind of apocalyptic terminology that leads exactly to an eschatological viewpoint. In conclusion, the fact that forgiveness of sins and of our brothers are the subject of the prayer that Jesus teaches shows that that prayer is the context in which forgiveness is applied and understood but not exhausted. It becomes a responsibility for the disciples called to build a fraternity into which God's mercy is joined and translated daily.

CHAPTER FOUR

The Gift of the Spirit and Forgiveness of Sins

Among the appearances of the Risen One narrated in the Gospel of John, Jesus' appearance to the disciples (see 20:19-23) is particularly important, because the gift of the Holy Spirit communicated to them and his words on the forgiveness of sins are crucial for the faith, life, and the future of the Christian community. Here, in fact, in an Easter context clearly connected to the death and resurrection of Jesus, the power to forgive or retain sins is delivered to the disciples as a task of their mandate, in close connection with the outpouring of the Holy Spirit.

The appearance of the risen Lord takes place "on the evening of that day, the first day of the week" (v. 19). It is the end of the day of Easter, which began with the discovery of the empty tomb, followed by the appearance of the Risen One to Mary Magdalene. Now the day reaches its climax because the Risen Christ is made present in the midst of the community of his disciples, sharing the gifts of his resurrection with them.

At the start of the story, to underscore the fact that the disciples are hidden all together in a house with locked doors, "for fear of the Jews," John juxtaposes the power acquired by the risen Lord who goes through those doors, showing his ability to overcome barriers and closures and to stand among them. With this strong contrast, the Gospel points out that the great hostility against Jesus does not end in his death but also extends to his community. Thus the Risen One reaches it, and nothing can prevent his presence and his proximity. This appearance leads the disciples to a new understanding and a new awareness of the faith they have placed in Jesus the Nazarene.

The Risen One first gives a greeting of peace and shows the signs of his passion: his hands and his wounded side. In the Old Testament, the greeting of peace was especially reserved for solemn moments and referred to the eschatological gift of peace, which would be the final one arising at the end of time by the work of God. In this sense, Jesus had already foretold this moment:

> "Peace I leave with you; my peace I give to you; not as the world gives do I give to you. Let not your hearts be troubled, neither let them be afraid. You heard me say to you, 'I go away, and I will come to you.' If you loved me, you would have rejoiced, because I go to the Father; for the Father is greater than I. And now I have told you before it takes place, so that when it does take place, you may believe." (Jn 14:27-29)

Now, peace comes to the disciples brought by the Risen Christ and confirmed by gestures that recall his death on the cross. Thus he shows the Eleven the continuity between crucifixion and resurrection. The One who is alive among them is the same Jesus who died crucified for them. They are immersed in a unique mystery of grace, participating in the Paschal Mystery. Through the Crucifixion Jesus manifested God's love for the world, and through his resurrection that love now triumphs over the powers that strive to lock man in fear. Jesus' Passover is the final saving event that brings the disciples the peace of God, and which causes them to rejoice, giving to the community of believers the certainty of the victory of Jesus Christ.

The greeting of peace is repeated in order to emphasize the new time that is opened up. In it resonates a mandate that puts the disciples in line with the mandate Christ received from the Father. The mission of the Church extends the saving mission of the Son who carries out the Father's plan. It is based on the authoritative word of the risen Lord and his powerful presence. It extends its scope and assumes its characteristics, sharing also difficulty and rejection. For this reason the disciples are given the gift of the Holy Spirit. The Risen One breathes on them (see v. 22), repeating the Creator's gesture (Gn 2:7).

In this new creation, the disciples are reborn as witnesses of the Risen Christ and, as such, are authorized to authoritatively proclaim the Gospel to the world. Through the Holy Spirit they are consecrated in the truth of Christ, just as Jesus had asked the Father in his farewell discourse: "Sanctify them in the truth; your word is truth. As you sent me into the world, so I have sent them into the world. And for their sake I consecrate myself, that they also may be consecrated in truth" (Jn 17:17-19).

The gift of the Spirit goes along with the words about the power to forgive and retain sins (see Jn 20:23). It is a verse that has caused large and lively debates, often threatening to reduce the richness of its meaning. In all the activities in which the Spirit given to them is present, the disciples receive the right to exercise a particular power over sin: in preaching, in testimony, in baptism and Eucharist, and also in what we now call sacramental penance. The Council of Trent uses this passage to affirm the institution of the Sacrament of Penance by Christ. Pope Francis sums up:

> Jesus, transfigured in his body, is already the new man who offers the Paschal gifts, the fruit of his death and resurrection. What are these gifts? Peace, joy, the forgiveness of sins, mission, but above all he gives the

Spirit who is the source of all these. The breath of Jesus, accompanied by the words with which he communicates the Spirit, signifies the transmission of life, the new life reborn from forgiveness. (General Audience, November 20, 2013)

On the day of his Passover, and as its fruit, the Risen One thus gave the assembled disciples the power to forgive sins.

Since the missionary mandate and the power to save are given to the community of the disciples as such, they remain valid. Their effectiveness does not end even after the Eleven have passed away but is passed on to their successors, the bishops. It is well known that the Sacrament of Penance has a long history, in which it has taken various forms, and the understanding of the sacrament has gradually increased. In it, the saving power against sin has never failed but instead has continued to flow copiously.

As Pope Francis reminds us:

This passage reveals to us the most profound dynamic contained in this sacrament. First, the fact that the forgiveness of our sins is not something we can give ourselves. I cannot say: I forgive my sins. Forgiveness is asked for, is asked of another, and in confession we ask for forgiveness from Jesus. Forgiveness is not the fruit of our own efforts but rather a gift; it is a gift of the Holy Spirit who fills us with the wellspring of mercy and of grace that flows unceasingly from the open heart of the Crucified and Risen Christ. Second, it reminds us that we can truly be at peace only if we allow ourselves to be reconciled, in the Lord Jesus, with the Father and with the brethren. (General Audience, February 19, 2014)

The power to forgive or to retain sins implies a judgment on the actions of the Christian and the sins perpetrated by them. Such discernment is carried out by the Church in two directions. It must expose and help believers to recognize sin in their lives so that they can put it behind them and reject it. At the same time, however, the Church welcomes the repentant sinner with open arms to entrust him once again to the salvific and creative word of Jesus. Thus the Church continues the work of her Lord:

> The Church is the depository of the power of the keys, of opening or closing to forgiveness. God forgives every man in his sovereign mercy, but he himself willed that those who belong to Christ and to the Church receive forgiveness by means of the ministers of the community. Through the apostolic ministry the mercy of God reaches me, my faults are forgiven and joy is bestowed on me. In this way Jesus calls us to live out reconciliation in the ecclesial, the community, dimension as well. And this is very beautiful. The Church, who is holy and at the same time in need of penitence, accompanies us on the journey of conversion throughout our life. The Church is not mistress of the power of the keys, but a servant of the ministry of mercy and rejoices every time she can offer this divine gift. (Pope Francis, General Audience, 20 November 2013)

The Sacrament of Penance is therefore intimately connected to baptism and the Eucharist, so that together, each in its own way, they actualize the sacrifice of Christ and its salvific reach for all believers:

> In the Sacrament of Baptism all sins are remitted, original sin and all of our personal sins, as well as the suffering of sin. With baptism the door to an effectively new life is opened, one which is not burdened by the weight of a negative past, but rather already feels the beauty and the goodness of the kingdom of heaven. It is

the powerful intervention of God's mercy in our lives, to save us. This saving intervention does not take away our human nature and its weakness — we are all weak and we are all sinners — and it does not take from us our responsibility to ask for forgiveness every time we err! I cannot be baptized many times, but I can go to confession and by doing so renew the grace of baptism. It is as though I were being baptized for a second time. The Lord Jesus is very very good and never tires of forgiving us. Even when the door that baptism opens to us in order to enter the Church is a little closed, due to our weaknesses and our sins. Confession reopens it, precisely because it is a second baptism that forgives us of everything and illuminates us to go forward with the light of the Lord. Let us go forward in this way, joyfully, because life should be lived with the joy of Jesus Christ; and this is a grace of the Lord. (Pope Francis, General Audience, November 13, 2013)

CHAPTER FIVE

The Words of Forgiveness

The formula of absolution of sins that the priest pronounces while extending his hands over the head of the penitent emphasizes the Trinitarian, Paschal, and ecclesial nature of the Sacrament of Penance. It offers the opportunity to outline a holistic vision of the sacrament.

God the Father of Mercies Has Reconciled the World to Himself

The first element is the mercy of the Father. The forgiveness of sins, in fact, stems from his free and firm will of salvation for the whole world. The whole history of salvation corresponds to the realization of this unique project. From the beginning, in fact, the history of the ancient people of God appears as the place of Yahweh's liberating action and the context in which he manifests himself as "merciful and gracious, / slow to anger and abounding in mercy and faithfulness" (Ps 86:15). The Exodus from Egypt and the Sinai Covenant sealed the mercy of God for his people. In it he presents himself as the Redeemer who liberates and saves, and the people become a holy people that in the covenant celebrates the foundation of its life and of its own identity. All of this allows the Christian to recognize God's pedagogy to his people. From it he can develop some fundamental attitudes for approaching the Sacrament of Reconciliation.

Because he springs from God's faithfulness, the Christian knows how important it is to *believe* in his mercy; it is a reconciling power that knows no insurmountable obstacles. Believing in this mercy means returning always to trust in the Father, in the certainty that the reality of sin in us is not greater than his mercy "in whatever our hearts condemn, for God is greater than our hearts and knows everything" (1 Jn 3:20, NABRE). For the believer, repentance, the desire and the guarantee of being forgiven, repairing the harm caused, are always possible because they rest on this unshakable certainty of faith, God's mercy, addressed to each person and the whole world. This means that no one saves himself: as God's unconditional gift, mercy must be requested and granted. It is the Father who reconciles to himself — the initiative is first of all his. The sacrament of forgiveness thus reminds the Christian sinner that he is part of a history of salvation that precedes him, a mercy into which he is inserted by grace and discovers the benevolent face of the Father, who repeatedly welcomes him in communion with him to the life of faith.

A second aspect: *mercy tends toward communion.* Mercy given by God rebuilds and strengthens relations weakened or broken by sin. It surrounds the penitent, opening space for the embrace of the Father and to the encounter with him. Forgiveness is not simply a gift given to the sinner independent from his will but aims to move his will to recognize in God a Father full of love, a love on which the life of faith is nourished for conversion. The absolution of sins is therefore not a mechanical, quasi-magical gesture. It is the grace that pervades the sinner by opening his heart, mind, and will to a life of communion with God.

One last note: in the Sacrament of Reconciliation, God's forgiveness reaches the Christian sinner *with the whole world in mind.* This means that the power of this forgiveness does not end in the encounter with the individual penitent, or with the Church alone.

God's mercy is indeed universal, even cosmic, since it is intimately connected to his will of salvation, which extends "to the whole creation" (Mk 16:15). As St. Paul reminds us, "creation itself will be set free from its bondage to decay and obtain the glorious liberty of the children of God" (Rom 8:21). The solidarity that unites the sinner to the world of corruption is thus superseded by the solidarity of redeeming grace. In it the Father's will powerfully reaches out to any place where the slavery of sin holds sway, so as to free the world from all its corruption.

In approaching the sacrament of forgiveness, Christians know they are involved in this powerful action. They receive the gift of forgiveness, but by the same token this gift involves them and pushes them forward within the project of liberation, which aims to reconcile all of creation to God. In receiving forgiveness, the repentant sinner keeps his gaze on his Lord, hears his word, and entrusts himself to it in order to build a world that, having sprung from that same Word, wants to return to it. Christian life is therefore a continuing *con-version* (turning toward) to that God whose heart always reaches out to sinful humanity and to the world in which it lives and that it builds.

In the Death and Resurrection of His Son

Solidarity and acceptance of sinners are traits that permeate the entire life of Jesus, whose very name means "Yahweh saves" (see Mt 1:21), from whose historical life comes God's forgiveness: "For the Son of man also came not to be served but to serve, and to give his life as a ransom for many" (Mk 10:45). The climax of this reconciliation accomplished by the Son of God is the offering of his life on the cross for all of us, when he begged and obtained the Father's forgiveness (Lk 23:34). Therefore, it is only in Christ the Redeemer that the fullness of God's forgiveness comes to man, and it is his Paschal Mystery that is at the center of salvation history.

From the cross of Christ, the forgiveness of sins comes permanently and continuously into the world, and by the power of the

Risen One it extends, eternally present into every place, "for many" (Mk 14:24). Since every sacrament is a particular manifestation of the presence of Christ's Passover in history, the redemption wrought by him reaches people in many and varied forms. The sacrament of forgiveness is first of all baptism, which gives man a new life. Since it is immersion in the death and resurrection of Jesus, baptism inserts the Christian into Christ's saving destiny. Thus it connects him to the new people journeying to the definitive Passover:

> But you are a chosen race, a royal priesthood, a holy nation, God's own people, that you may declare the wonderful deeds of him who called you out of darkness into his marvelous light. Once you were no people but now you are God's people; once you had not received mercy but now you have received mercy. (1 Pt 2:9-10)

For the baptized, all this involves a new way of living: "We were buried therefore with him by baptism into death, so that as Christ was raised from the dead by the glory of the Father, we too might walk in newness of life" (Rom 6:4).

The new life of baptism, however, does not negate the frailty of human nature, so the path of the Christian is still marked by the painful experience of sin and demands the continuous renewal of God's forgiveness in the Sacrament of Reconciliation. In it Christ's victory over sin becomes historical and visible to everyone through the Church. The repetition of the celebration of this sacrament of healing shows all the renewing power of that dynamism of salvation, which God set irreversibly into human history with the incarnation, death, and resurrection of Jesus. Reconciled with God in Christ, the baptized is thus constantly transfigured by the Passover of the Lord who is the solidity from which he begins to live "in," "with," and "for" Christ (see Eph 2:10; Col 3:3; Rom 6:8; Phlm 1:6). The relationship with Christ thus constitutes his existence, and from it he understands himself, humanity, the world, history.

Illuminated by faith and enlivened by the love that comes from the glorious cross of the Lord, he is set free and courageous in front of everyone and everything and, for this reason, evangelically protagonist and responsible in the Church and in the world. Moved by faith, the believer learns not only to see Christ in human beings so as to be open to charity in solidarity, but also to see human beings "in Christ," in order to understand them in their fullness and commit himself to their full development.

And He Sent the Holy Spirit for the Remission of Sins

The forgiveness of sins caused by Jesus' death on the cross reaches every Christian by virtue of the Holy Spirit poured out by God through the Risen Christ. It is the Spirit, in fact, who implements the effectiveness of the Passover of Jesus within the Christian community. Otherwise, it would be an event of the past, far away in time, and it could not be implemented in the sacramental sign to be communicated to believers. The Holy Spirit, therefore, appears as a force that allows the fulfillment of the saving plan of the Father carried out by the Son.

The Gospels show that the Spirit of God — that is, the life and power of God — acts first of all in Jesus, in his earthly life. Starting from the baptism in the Jordan (see Mt 3:13-17; Mk 1:9-11; Lk 3:21-22) Jesus began his public ministry and continues it, characterized by the intimate bond and filled with the Spirit, which is God, as the Father. In the synagogue of Nazareth (Lk 4:16-19), Jesus proclaims that the prophecy of Isaiah 61:1-2 is fulfilled in him. He is the Anointed One, and the one sent by the "Spirit of the Lord" in charge of bringing the good news to the poor, to proclaim release to the captives, to give sight to the blind, and to set free those who are oppressed by inaugurating the year of the Lord's favor. So all the activity of Jesus is under the sign of the Holy Spirit.

The risen Lord gives the same Spirit to his community. As the life-giving power of God and the beginning of the new creation, he lives in the Church and enables her to accomplish the mission entrusted to her by the Lord. In this he gives the apostles the power to forgive sins, thus fulfilling in the Church and through her Christ's work aimed at reconciliation between man and God. In this way the Spirit intimately unites the baptized in Christ and, at the same time, believers among themselves in the Church. In the ritual of the Sacrament of Penance the role of the Holy Spirit is greatly emphasized. He is repeatedly mentioned by showing that all the action is under his sign: Before, during, and after the celebration, the Spirit accompanies and always acts upon both the penitent and the minister of the sacrament. Above all, the Holy Spirit is at the origin of the process of conversion, because he urges the sinner to repent and return to the Lord. He fulfills what the Psalmist already invoked: "Restore us, O God; let thy face shine, that we may be saved!" (Ps 80:3).

The Spirit, about which the hymn *Veni Creator Spiritus* proclaims, "Kindle our sense from above, / And make our hearts o'erflow with love," also gives the gift of the truth in our consciences and, with it, gives the assurance of the forgiveness of sins. Therefore, in welcoming the sinner, the priest recalls the active presence of the Holy Spirit in him and in the Church: "May God, who has enlightened every heart, help you to know your sins and trust in his mercy." This admonition, one of the approved formulas, shows that the penitent must not only discern his sins, but also come to *metanoia*, conversion of heart. As an action moved by the Spirit of Truth who is also the Spirit of Love, in the intimacy of conscience, the examination of one's life becomes at the same time a new beginning where the grace of love of God, and of our brethren, is bestowed upon us.

As the minister of the sacrament acts in the name of Christ and of the Church, the Holy Spirit extends its action on him: "Priest and penitents should prepare themselves above all by prayer to celebrate the sacrament. The priest should call upon the Holy Spirit so that he may receive enlightenment and charity" (*Rite of Penance*, 15). "Enlightenment" and "charity" mean recognizing discernment and mercy as gifts of the Spirit. The same ritual of penance furnishes further details:

> In order that he may fulfill his ministry properly and faithfully, understand the disorders of souls and apply the appropriate remedies to them, and act as a wise judge.... For the discernment of spirits is indeed a deep knowledge of God's working in the human heart, a gift of the Spirit, and an effect of charity.... By receiving repentant sinners and leading them to the light of the truth, the confessor fulfills a paternal function: he reveals the heart of the Father and reflects the image of Christ the Good Shepherd. He should keep in mind that he has been entrusted with the ministry of Christ, who accomplished the saving work of human redemption by mercy and by his power present in the sacraments. (10)

Since the Spirit of Christ brings about the remission of sins, the exercise of this ministry can only be inspired, supported, and guided by the same Spirit. In this way, the Sacrament of Penance qualifies as a privileged manifestation of the presence of the Spirit in the Church, so that the plan of salvation in history reaches its fullness. It is a "wonder of salvation."

Through the Ministry of the Church

The remission of sins, obtained through the death and resurrection of Christ, takes effect over time through the action of the Holy Spirit and reaches the Christian sinner in the Church and through the Church. The ecclesial dimension of the sacrament is constitutive, although difficult to understand. Even today many, in fact, understand sin as something exclusively individual.

Since the Sacrament of Penance celebrates the merciful love of God toward man and the loving response of the repentant sinner to

God, the mediating action of the Church develops in both directions. Also, because forgiveness is accomplished "in Christ" and "in the Church," in addition to being a return to God, it is also a return to the Church community.

In *Lumen Gentium*, the Second Vatican Council speaks of the reconciliation between the sinner and the Church by affirming the simultaneity of the reconciliation with God. In this document, the first to deal with this issue officially, the Church is described as a community enlivened by the Holy Spirit, and therefore sin is always a contradiction that wounds her nature. The action of the Spirit reaches out, therefore, to bring the repentant sinner into the fullness of the Church community in order to restore the integrity of the communion that has been violated: "Those who approach the sacrament of Penance obtain pardon from the mercy of God for the offense committed against him and are at the same time reconciled with the Church, which they have wounded by their sins, and which by charity, example, and prayer seeks their conversion" (*Lumen Gentium*, 11). The *Catechism of the Catholic Church* takes up this theme:

> This sacrament *reconciles us with the Church*. Sin damages or even breaks fraternal communion. The sacrament of Penance repairs or restores it. In this sense it does not simply heal the one restored to ecclesial communion, but has also a revitalizing effect on the life of the Church which suffered from the sin of one of her members. (1469)

St. John Paul II particularly highlighted the far-ranging reconciliation brought about by God. This reconciliation, in fact, heals much damage caused by sin, from the inner being of the sinner all the way to his relationship with creation:

> But it has to be added that this reconciliation with God leads, as it were, to other reconciliations which repair the

breaches caused by sin. The forgiven penitent is reconciled with himself in his inmost being, where he regains
his own true identity. He is reconciled with his brethren
whom he has in some way attacked and wounded. He
is reconciled with the church. He is reconciled with all
creation. (*Reconciliatio et Paenitentia*, 31)

The ecclesial context also helps to better understand why the
forgiveness of sins is linked to the absolution of the priestly ministry. The Sacrament of Reconciliation implies first of all the exercise
of the priesthood of the whole Church, both the common priesthood and the ministerial priesthood. The common priesthood of the
faithful is exercised primarily by the penitent. He does not passively
live reconciliation, but, urged on by grace, he cooperates actively in
his own conversion and full reintegration into the communion of
the Church. Nor does the ecclesial community passively experience
the penitent's reintegration but rather contributes to his conversion "by charity, example, and prayer." The whole Church therefore
exercises its common priesthood so as to achieve the reconciliation
and pardon of her sinful children. In this sense the support that she
offers such as correction, discernment, help, and encouragement
along the penitential journey are precious expressions of her "charity," because they aid reintegration into ecclesial charity.

The exercise of the common priesthood, however, requires the
exercise of the ministerial priesthood that is at its service. As minister of confession, the priest imparts sacramental grace "in Christ"
and "in the Church," two points that clarify the exercise of his
ministry and at the same time set its boundaries. Acting "in the
name of Christ and by the power of the Holy Spirit" (*Rite of Penance*, 9), the minister is at the service of the word of the Lord since
he implements the mandate of the forgiveness of sins that Christ
entrusted to the apostles and their successors. The bishop is thus
the moderator of the penitential discipline and full holder of the
ministry of reconciliation, which he administers by entrusting it

also to his priest collaborators. This is a power that cannot in any way be exercised in an arbitrary manner but only in accordance with the teachings and intentions of Christ: "The confessor is not the master of God's forgiveness, but its servant. The minister of this sacrament should unite himself to the intention and charity of Christ" (*Catechism*, 1466). At the same time, the priest also acts "in the name of the Church," in the service of the ecclesial communion to which reconciliation with God leads. It follows that the exercise of the ministry of reconciliation must be exercised in communion and harmony with the Church and her magisterium. For this reason the *Catechism* recommends the following about the minister:

> He should have a proven knowledge of Christian behavior, experience of human affairs, respect and sensitivity toward the one who has fallen; he must love the truth, be faithful to the Magisterium of the Church, and lead the penitent with patience toward healing and full maturity. He must pray and do penance for his penitent, entrusting him to the Lord's mercy. (1466)

Pardon and Peace

Peace is the final outcome of the saving action arising from the mercy of the Father. It is the fruit of forgiveness and reconciliation with God obtained through confession of our sins. It is not simply the psychological peace that the penitent may feel after "lightening" the heart from the burden of his sins, but it is biblical peace, God's gift, a visible sign of his covenant. It is the "new" peace that has its foundations in the death and resurrection of Jesus and that overcomes every tearing away from God and our brothers. It is the peace that the Holy Spirit instills in the disciples of the Lord by giving them the courage and vitality for the proclamation and witness of the Gospel.

In the long farewell discourse (see Jn 13-17), Jesus unites the gift of peace to the Holy Spirit the Comforter (Jn 14:25-31). The

Spirit "will teach you all things," and that teaching is intimately connected to the teaching of Jesus, because he will "bring to your remembrance all that I have said to you" (Jn 14:26). The task of the Spirit is to carry on and keep alive the history of the revelation of Jesus, not because we add new things, but because it continually deepens our understanding of revelation. Its action allows every Christian community to live faithfulness to the Gospel in its own time.

The repentant sinner is forgiven and therefore reached by the gift of peace, the reflection of the eschatological and definitive salvation that God offers to humanity in Christ Jesus, and truly within him by sacramental grace. It is this peace that sustains Christians in the vicissitudes of life and trials that they meet in witnessing to the faith. It is "his peace," the peace of Christ who announces the Gospel and sends the Spirit. The richness of this salvation is described in the Gospel of John as a reality of many complementary facets. It is "truth," "light," "life," "peace," and "joy." God's forgiveness introduces us to all these things. Wrapped in the Father's mercy, reached by the paschal mystery of Christ, supported by the strength of the Holy Spirit, the repentant sinner is disposed to receive the absolution of sins that introduces him to the peace of God.

And I Absolve You from Your Sins in the Name of the Father and of the Son and of the Holy Spirit

The gesture of laying on of hands by which the priest accompanies the words of absolution signifies the outpouring of the Holy Spirit for the forgiveness of sins, reconciliation, and communion with the Lord. The Sacrament of Penance, in fact, not only brings about the "cancellation" of sins but also aims to arouse in the one who receives it the will to change his mentality and orientation of life, a way of conversion that only the Holy Spirit can initiate and support. The words of absolution are laden with solemnity and authority. The initial "I" emphatically points out that the one who is speaking does not do so in his own name but as the depository of that authority to forgive sins that the Lord entrusted to the apostles and their successors. It also expresses the faith and the participation of the whole Church, which is involved in the reconciliation of the penitent, affirming above all that the pronunciation of absolution is not a simple statement of God's forgiveness but is the effective word which forgives sins because in it and in union with the minister the Father, the Son, and Holy Spirit are acting. The penitent is thus truly immersed in the saving action of God that regenerates him to the grace of baptism.

CHAPTER SIX

The Sacrament of Reconciliation in Pastoral Ministry

The call for vigilance and fortitude in faith conclude the First Letter to the Corinthians: "Be watchful, stand firm in your faith" (16:13). Watchfulness, often associated with prayer and sobriety (see 1 Thes 5:6), is the hallmark of the Christian who lives in expectation of the Lord. Staying firm in the faith designates the constant and stable commitment to live the relationship with the Lord.

All this aims to reinforce the profound commitment of the believer in the Gospel, an adherence that is always threatened by external difficulties and inner disturbances. To these first two recommendations St. Paul adds three more, "Be courageous, be strong. Let all that you do be done in love" (1 Cor 16:13-14). The apostle condenses into these expressions a real-life program whose unifying center is the love of God. It is an appeal to the courage, confidence, and firmness that are required of those who face a struggle. Yes, because the Christian life is a struggle and a battle: "You then, my son, be strong in the grace that is in Christ Jesus. Take your share of suffering as a good soldier of Christ Jesus" (2 Tm 2:1,3).

With respect to a ministry aimed at valuing the Sacrament of Reconciliation in an ecclesial and social context as complex as today's, we should point out and seriously consider certain qualifying points that are both central and fundamental but also dynamic because they are capable of enhancing and shaping personalities and Christian experiences in many directions.

1. The Formation of Conscience

The Sacrament of Reconciliation is premised on the need to form consciences. The expression refers to faith that becomes knowledge. The term "conscience" (from the Latin *con-scientia*, in Greek *syn-eidesis*) refers to a knowledge that is not the result of individual efforts but a knowing "together." In Christian tradition, this meaning is taken in a broad sense and refers not only to the light of grace that allows us to recognize our sins. For the Christian, it instead means understanding the significance of what happens, especially in one's life, in an understanding that is realized together with God and through him. The Christian life is fulfilled in the Holy Spirit, by Christ's love, illuminated by his word. For the believer, knowledge of self and of the world is therefore a work of spiritual discernment.

Today care for the formation of consciences is a more urgent task than ever. Every believer should take responsibility for it, and confessors, spiritual directors, parents, and all educators should reserve special attention for it, in general. It is, in fact, easy to see that in our society, so often marked by serious phenomena of human and even moral degradation, too many consciences are muffled by public opinion, almost dormant or resigned in a kind of irenic wishful thinking, assuming that in the end it is enough to be "pretty good" — "do not kill and do not steal," "do not hurt anyone" — and then tell the confessor, "the rest is up to you." The inability to undertake an examination of one's conscience is a serious contradiction of people of our time. It is a kind of disease which prevents the enlightening grace given by the Holy Spirit to act, and it obscures the understanding of the true dignity of man and prevents the discovery of the truth of our own sin so that it can be forgiven.

Calling it "God's voice in us," ancient tradition has seen in the conscience man's participation in God. With this concept the inviolable character of conscience is also enshrined, placing it above any human law. The need for such a direct link between God and man gives him not only an absolute dignity, but also full freedom against all that is coercive or tries to manipulate his choices. It is because God makes himself present to conscience that it becomes an instrument of human freedom which, sustained by grace, seeks the true and the good. As a tool within man, in order to become what it is, it needs to grow, to be formed, to practice. So as not to shrink or become deformed, it needs the help of others, the Word of God alive in its uninterrupted transmission, frank and loyal advice, silence and reflection, and prayer. Conscience requires training and education. It reveals our identity and generates a lifestyle. It indicates personal maturity and sensitivity to moral and social appeals. Conversely, loss or silence of the conscience may become the disease that poisons not only the life of faith but an entire civilization.

How is conscience formed? By setting on a path that goes into the truth about man, the one who is the image of God. In this context, recognizing our sins (all sin is a falsifying vision of self, others, the world, and God) is only a stage on this great journey of knowledge of self and God. It is a path that is very challenging but at the same time beautiful and compelling.

The *Catechism of the Catholic Church* reminds us that conscience is formed, educated, upright, and true when it is "in conformity with the true good willed by the wisdom of the Creator" (1783), and that this education "is a lifelong task" (1784). Knowledge of God illuminates the knowledge of oneself. In fact, the person is never fully conscious of himself except when in relationship with God. This knowledge "with God" is to know oneself in Christ through the light of the Holy Spirit. This is a knowledge which "guarantees freedom and engenders peace of heart" (*Catechism*, 1784). The formation of conscience is therefore born and developed by the encounter with Christ, is illuminated and nourished by his word, and causes us to do the works that the Spirit suggests. Faith is not without works, and redemption is not without sanctification. Conscience, therefore, matures within a positive and realistic vision of the human condition, which exposes every false image of God and of oneself. To learn to discern means to practice examining and evaluation. Ultimately, it means keeping our center of gravity in Christ, not in ourselves, letting the grace of God work and act in us and through us. Then we remain vigilant in recognizing what doesn't make us free, what creates disorder in us, and what is therefore not ordered to our vocation as children of God.

Priests, as confessors and spiritual directors to whom the faithful open their consciences and whom are asked for enlightened advice, have the great responsibility, linked to their own ministry, to be masters of the spiritual life. So they themselves need a careful education in the discernment of spirits. Beginning with seminary training, such an education needs to grow and be refined in the exercise of ministry as well as through comparison with their confreres on the current needs of society, the major problems they encounter in the education of consciences, and the common guidelines to be emphasized. For priests, as for all believers, it should be clear that conscience is formed when it takes the form of Christ, taking on his feelings and making his style its own.

Where to begin? With attention to concrete things. Pope Francis has urged believers to resume the ancient "but very good" practice of examination of conscience. It "is a grace, because to guard our heart is to guard the Holy Spirit, who is within us" (Homily, October 10, 2014). The Spirit spurs believers to embody the word of salvation in everyday life. It is not about making big speeches or high speculation, such as: "Well done, good and faithful servant; you have been faithful over a little, I will set you over much; enter into the joy of your master" (Mt 25:21). Conscience is formed as it watches and casts light. It does not stop at recognizing sin, but discerns the thoughts and feelings that produce it, thoughts and feelings that are often our most hidden impulses. It is by observing concrete particulars that the Christian can grasp where and to whom or what he is pushed — he understands who he is becoming. Thus it is in the encounter with Christ who saves, in prayer and in listening to his Word, in the relationship with the ecclesial community, in comparison with others and with the world around him, that the sinner finds his own image as a beloved and forgiven son. He then comes to be a son in the Son, and this recognition creates the desire of a more happy life.

2. Educating to the Meaning of Penance

To Christian communities and individual believers, the Jubilee of Mercy stands out as a good opportunity to rediscover the value and beauty of the Sacrament of Reconciliation. It is desirable that in pastoral-year programs there be planned catechetical meetings and initiatives that, starting from the theme of God's mercy, help to outline an appropriate framework for promoting the faithful's approach to this sacrament. All efforts, as laudable as they may be, will not be sufficient, nor give lasting fruit, if we as Church do not pose the higher question of how to educate today to the sense of penance. There is no doubt that in our day it has been declining, so that many are completely missing the penitential dimension of Christian life. Gradually but surely, such a loss dissolves the sense of the gratuity of grace and thus leads to neglect, if not to abandonment, of the sacraments in general and that of reconciliation in particular.

When man no longer recognizes himself as a sinner he does nothing to avoid sin or to eliminate it, and the grace of salvation for him becomes negligible. In such a case, the believer loses the awareness of Easter and the reason for the Lord's death on the cross. His life of faith is emptied, devitalized, without enthusiasm, a sad habit of life. On the contrary, Christian asceticism speaks of the sense of penance as a "spiritual struggle" in which the heart, the mind, and the will of the disciple remain vigilant and attentive, a necessary way to strengthen the personality of the believer, a test to concretely measure the "quality" of his relationship with the Lord, and above all a joyful response to the grace that God bestows profusely. In this sense an autobiographical passage of St. Paul is enlightening:

> But whatever gain I had, I counted as loss for the sake of Christ. Indeed I count everything as loss because of the surpassing worth of knowing Christ Jesus my Lord. For his sake I have suffered the loss of all things, and count them as refuse, in order that I may gain Christ and be found in him.... Not that I have already obtained this or am already perfect; but I press on to make it my own, because Christ Jesus has made me his own. (Phil 3:7-12)

Reviving the feelings of affection and gratitude to the Christians of Philippi, the first Macedonian community he founded in Europe, the apostle, now old and a prisoner in Rome, wrote a letter to strengthen the bond of charity and love that bound him to them. He covertly alludes to the experience of Damascus, an event that led him to faith in Christ, and reveals how he has operated in its grace and how great is the new life that flows from it. From that moment on, what had been a great gain appeared to him as "refuse," and now he is striving "in order that I may gain Christ and be found in him" (see vv. 8,9).

It is precisely this strong and wonderful striving that we need to rediscover. The sense of penance opens the conscience to a sense of sin, brings forth the pain for our flaws, urges us to repair the evil committed, disposes us to entrust ourselves with a generous heart to all the good that the Lord inspires in order to always be "in Christ." The episode of Damascus reoriented the life of Paul, and he then acted in order to be able to "gain" — that is, conquer — Christ who appeared to him. "Conquer" is the verb of lovers: Will the lover be able to conquer his beloved? All that he had thus far lived with great intensity is judged loss, because there is something more important that it urges. It is essential to "gain Christ." And you gain when you are "found in him." For the apostle, the Law used to be at the center and was followed by the obedience due to it. In the new universe, the Risen Christ is now the center.

One last step: After knowing and conforming to, there is "running" (v. 12). Paul wants to conquer Jesus because he was conquered by him. Faith is re-cognition: a return to know the one who is already known. On the one hand it is the continuous revelation, on the other hand the continuous re-knowing. It is, in short, an inexhaustible, dynamic, and challenging relationship.

Christians know that they have never arrived. They run regardless of age, strength and energy, successes and failures. They run in history, as Paul did throughout the Mediterranean, wherever Christ wants to be met and wherever humanity manifests the face of the Crucified One, or thirsts for consoling words, or stretches out its hands in hope, or is disfigured in its dignity. Christians run and hurry, forgetting what lies behind the hardships, misunderstandings, failures, seeking only the goal of always being all "found in Christ." After all, the penitential dimension of Christian life only helps us to place the center of gravity of our lives in Christ, not in ourselves, letting the grace of God work and act in us and through us.

St. John Paul II explained it this way: "Here it is a question of acquiring again the simplicity of thought, of will, and of heart which is indispensable to meet God in one's own 'self'" (General Audience, Ash Wednesday, February 28, 1979). In true repentance the only action is to make space for his action in us. This is exactly the dynamic that characterizes every genuine relationship of love: "Love is indeed 'ecstasy,' not in the sense of a moment of intoxication, but rather as a journey, an ongoing exodus out of the closed inward-looking self towards its liberation through self-giving, and thus towards authentic self-discovery and indeed the discovery of God" (Pope Benedict XVI, *Deus Caritas Est*, 6). It is the road that leads us directly to seek and to love the Sacrament of Penance.

The *Catechism of the Catholic Church* lists many forms of penance and penitential attitudes that favor conversion, which the pastoral imagination can draw on to form suggestions to individuals and communities, from the most classic of fasting, prayer, and almsgiving, to other invitations described as practices of charity, gestures of reconciliation, concern for the poor, commitment in defense of justice and rights, fraternal correction, reading of sacred Scripture, spiritual exercises, penitential liturgies, and pilgrimages (see 1434-38).

3. Living Reconciliation

God's forgiveness is not confined to the repentant sinner, but through him it radiates throughout the community by transforming interpersonal relationships and imparting to the whole Church a lifestyle that characterizes her as "people of God." The Letter to the Ephesians calls passionately:

> And do not grieve the Holy Spirit of God, in whom you were sealed for the day of redemption. Let all bitterness and wrath and anger and clamor and slander be put away from you, with all malice, and be kind to one another, tenderhearted, forgiving one another, as God in Christ forgave you. (4:30-32)

The expression "grieve the Holy Spirit" recalls a text of Isaiah that condemns the attitude of rebellion of the Israelites to the Lord who had saved them with "love" and "pity" (see Is 63:8-10). In doing so they deny their identity as the Chosen People, redeemed by the love of God. Through the allusion to Isaiah, Ephesians reminds Christians that through baptism they were included in the saving plan of God through the gift of the Spirit; therefore reprehensible conduct contradicts the gift received and the redemptive action of God. To grieve the Spirit means not to allow him to carry it out, and that happens when you violate the requirements of brotherly love. Instead they are called to a responsible attitude of cooperation with the saving plan of God, which unfolds in history. Therefore, believers are urged to first remove from the ecclesial community all those events in opposition to the solidarity that must reign in it.

In this passage from the Letter to the Ephesians, five synonyms belonging to the semantics of wrath are arranged to reveal a certain progression in attitudes that undermine relationships, breaking the brotherhood of faith. It is behavior incompatible with the status of new men received in baptism. They must dwell in that same generosity and magnanimity that God has shown to them in Christ. Thus comes the invitation to adopt attitudes of reciprocal acceptance culminating in mutual forgiveness. The motivation appears at the end of the verse — the believer can accept and forgive because he knows that first he has been unconditionally accepted and forgiven by God. Forgiveness is therefore a free gift received in order to be shared with the brethren. Such a deep self-awareness of faith makes solidarity the dominant feature of the Christian community, both in its own internal relations and in the way it faces the world. In living the reconciliation granted to her by God, with the help of the Holy Spirit, the Church becomes its announcer and dispenser to the world. In it her witness shines.

St. Paul reminds the Galatians what it means to live in the world animated by the Spirit of the Risen One: "But the fruit of the Spirit is love, joy, peace, patience, kindness, goodness, faithfulness, gentleness, self-control" (Gal 5:22-23). The list shows the path that the Spirit marks out for believers. The result is unique and creates unity in the new life of the Christian. It appears, however, in different forms: first, *agape*, the generous love that comes from God. It brings the *joy* that is the strongest aspiration of the heart of man, created to be loved and to love. And together with joy it also brings the *peace* that puts us in accord with the will of God and allows us to overcome unrest and conflict because it orients everyone toward goodness and harmony. The list continues with more specific aspects: *patience* that knows how to wait and endure, *kindness* that predisposes us to encounter others, *goodness* that opens us to service, *faithfulness* that makes us persevere and be relied upon, *gentleness* that excludes the use of violent means, and *self-control* against all forms of debauchery and anger. All these aspects of the "fruit" of the Spirit pertain to the believer in his relations with others and therefore constitute a sort of examination of conscience for all Christian communities.

The action of the grace of God's forgiveness is not fulfilled if we do not find ways to make the Spirit fruitful in life's concreteness. The areas where acts of reconciliation are needed are truly endless and occupy the whole of existence and human activity: from personal life, where alienating situations exist to varying degrees, to the relationships between couples struggling to express genuine love; from family reality increasingly undermined in its identity, to generational relations where conflicts and misunderstandings occur; from the labor market and the economy undergoing crises and profound conflicts, to the social situation where neediness and poverty emerge ever more; from the political situation so often built on partial interests, to the international context marked by the power of the rich nations over the poor ones; from wars that set fire to many parts of the world, to the divisions between Christians and misunderstandings between believers of different faiths. It is in this vast and articulated program that the whole Church, in all her communities and all her faithful, is called to offer the testimony of a life reconciled and service of reconciliation:

> To the extent that Christians are grateful and faithful to God's great gift of reconciliation they have received, they become living witnesses and sources of reconciliation in everyday life. Reconciliation with God is thus a source of fraternal reconciliation — in the ecclesial community and in human society — which together are the grace received but also the responsibility that Christians assume towards the world. The tensions and divisions that continue to weigh on the world — the great and the small worlds into which Christians as individuals and

communities are inserted — thus become a challenge for those who have received the gift of reconciliation. Those who have been freed from sin by the grace of Christ can be, together with all people of good will, agents of justice and peace in the world. (Italian Episcopal Conference, *Reconciliation and Penance in the Mission of the Church*, 42)

The service of reconciliation is a call that concerns each of us, a call that is always relevant at all levels and in spite of the complexity of division. Some urgent points should be highlighted, however.

Reconciliation Within the Community

It is within the Christian community that the theme of reconciliation must first be addressed. The unity that characterizes the Church is not the result of more or less successful efforts of its members, nor is it given by canon law imposed or discipline gained from the tradition. Unity is an original fact. In baptism, Christians are incorporated into Christ, members of his body, living believers in the believing community that lives in Christ. It is from that original unity, recognized as a gift received, that Christians learn to seek and to live communion and reconciliation with our brethren. It rests on faith knowing that no grievance, no misunderstanding, no difference (of culture, race, political opinion, social class, etc.) is sufficient reason to separate from Christ and thus from his body, which is the Church. Indeed, contrary to all evidence, this unity must always be believed and confessed as the most typical expression of faith in the crucified and risen Lord. It must also constantly be safeguarded through two basic attitudes, the search for those who are estranged and brotherly correction.

a) Seeking Out the Missing

It may seem obvious, but in the Christian community there is always someone who is missing, and sometimes this absence is discouraging to the remaining few. Even among the larger communities there are always empty seats left by those who distance themselves. We are wounded brotherhoods.

In the parable of the lost sheep, Jesus introduces the story with a question, "What man of you, having a hundred sheep, if he has lost one of them, does not leave the ninety-nine in the wilderness, and go after the one which is lost, until he finds it?" (Lk 15:4). Commentators typically start from the shepherd's action and end by highlighting the joy at the finding of the lost sheep. Sometimes, however, we should also assume the vantage point of the flock, abandoned by the shepherd in a desert with no fences, defenseless, without any care, all in order to seek out just one. Left alone, what will happen to the ninety-nine? They will be afraid, they will seek refuge, but in the desert they will have no other defense than to follow the shepherd who is already on the move. Their safety is not in being enclosed but in being where their shepherd is, and their shepherd will be where they find the lost sheep.

Following the Risen One is invariably a journey of brotherhood for all. In Jesus' vision, as in that of the Church, there is no loss of sheep to which you resign yourself. There are only sheep that are "found" and returned to the community of the brethren. No distance can keep the shepherd away; no flock can therefore give up on a brother. We have no alternative: the Shepherd must be sought where he wants to be found, where his joy is full.

b) Brotherly Correction

The Jubilee of Mercy is meant to be a reconciliation above all within the Christian community; a mission *ad intra*, a journey of discovery and conversion within the Church's identity as the universal community of salvation, so that the Gospel may reach the whole person in every person. On this path "brotherly correction" plays a particularly important role and one not easy to implement. Pope Francis has recognized this:

"Take aside your brother who made the error and speak
to him.".... And "to take him aside," indeed, means "to
correct him with charity." It would be like "performing
surgery without anesthesia," resulting in a patient's
painful death. And "charity is like an aesthesia which
helps him to receive the care and to accept the correction.".... "The truth" is always needed, even if at times
"it isn't good to hear it." In every case if the truth "is
told with charity and with love, it is easier to accept."
(*L'Osservatore Romano* reporting on September 12, 2014,
Homily at Santa Martha)

In his exhortation to the Galatians, St. Paul examines the problem of how to deal with a community member who commits a fault:
"Brethren, if a man is overtaken in any trespass, you who are spiritual should restore him in a spirit of gentleness. Look to yourself,
lest you too be tempted" (Gal 6:1). Instead of a strict reprimand,
the apostle suggests gentleness, basing this attitude on the awareness of our own moral weakness and hence the risk, anything but
hypothetical, of being tempted ourselves. To correct in a spirit of
gentleness means to set someone back on course. The rehabilitation
of the brother who sins is therefore the task of the whole community, without excluding the fact that each person must examine
his conscience in order to not fall in turn. Paul calls the Galatians
"spiritual" (*oi pneumatikoi*) — that is, living by the Spirit and therefore called to act according to the Spirit and to guarantee the community their "spiritual" help. The call to reconciliation is therefore
a call to action that applies to all believers. The whole community
has received the Spirit and is thus rendered capable of leading to
conversion those who fall into error and sin.

Brotherly correction aims exactly at reconciliation in order to
build up the community. Speaking of the first Christian communities, the letters of the New Testament offer many expressions of
solidarity, in which the bond with one another is a recurring theme.

The framework in which brotherly correction can be exercised is thus delineated: outdo one another in showing honor (see Rom 12:10), live in harmony with one another (Rom 12:16), welcome one another (Rom 15:7), wait for one another (1 Cor 11:33), through love be servants of one another (Gal 5:13), bear one another's burdens (Gal 6:2), encourage one another (1 Thes 5:11), be at peace among yourselves (1 Thes 5:13), seek to do good to one another (1 Thes 5:15), forbear one another in love (Eph 4:2), be kind to one another and tenderhearted (Eph 4:32), be subject to one another (Eph 5:21), forgive each other (Col 3:13), pray for one another (James 5:16), love one another earnestly (1 Pt 1:22), practice hospitality ungrudgingly to one another (1 Pt 4:9), clothe yourselves with humility toward one another (1 Pt 5:5), have fellowship with one another (1 Jn 1:7).

Reconciliation presupposes a mutual collaboration, a coming together with one another. Brotherly correction activates the conscience of each individual so that conversion becomes the powerful engine of the journey of the Christian community. "So we are ambassadors for Christ, God making his appeal through us. We beg you on behalf of Christ, be reconciled to God" (2 Cor 5:20). Thus, for all, the mission of reconciliation is summed up and embodied in being "eager to maintain the unity of the Spirit in the bond of peace" (Eph 4:3). Penitential celebrations in preparation for individual confession have excellent reference points in these steps for a review of community life.

Architects of Reconciliation in the World

The service of reconciliation that the Church is called to play in the world is neither easy nor painless, for the Church herself first of all. The cause is not only the complexity and scope of this mission, but the deep contrast between the Gospel of forgiveness and the logic of the world. Since reconciliation flows from the Cross, it makes us participants in the mystery of the redemptive death of Christ. Revealing the dynamics with which the Lord's salvation extends throughout the world, the Book of Revelation attests the otherness between the announcement of the Gospel and the world's mindset, to the point that by the mere fact of belonging to Christ believers are open to trial and persecution in every age. Through baptism the life of the Christian becomes witness (Greek *martyría*) of the Gospel of salvation for reconciliation and peace among men. It is an irrevocable commitment. The Church is not a community of heroes and daredevils, yet she does not flee in trials and persecution. She invokes the Holy Spirit, the Spirit of peace and reconciliation, to save her life if that corresponds to God's plan and, in any case, invokes the gift of *parresía* — that is, the force of freedom and frankness on behalf of the Gospel.

The image of the apostles Peter and John with the whole community, in the midst of persecution, raising praise to the Lord is memorable: "And now, Lord, look upon their threats, and grant to your servants to speak your word with all boldness" (Acts 4:29). After the prayer, "The place in which they were gathered together was shaken; and they were all filled with the Holy Spirit and spoke the word of God with boldness" (v. 31). Even when it does not reach the point of martyrdom, the witness of reconciliation means to enter the field of play with a humble but tenacious presence, even willing to personally pay the price of Jesus. The inevitable conflicts arising from sin involve renewing the struggle to try to understand one another, a careful distinction between what is essential and what is part of a legitimate difference of opinion. It implies respect and understanding and also taking on a new mentality on which to base the relationship between people, a mentality centered on the love the Spirit of God pours into those who love Jesus.

But when every road of reconciliation seems to be blocked, what can a Christian do? From Abraham to Moses, to the Psalms, to Jesus on the cross, the biblical tradition shows the power of intercessory prayer. Interceding is not just praying for someone, but, as suggested by the etymology of "stepping into the midst," it means to place oneself within a situation. Interceding means to stand where the conflict takes place and, without moving, remain between the two parties in confrontation. Intercessory prayer extends its arms to both sides to unite, reconcile, and pacify. It is the gesture of Jesus on the cross, a gesture in which the Son of God himself reconciles the incurable human situation to God. Born in prayer, the Church lives it and steadfastly believes in its effectiveness. For that reason she prays every day for the forgiveness of the sins of all her children and for the conversion of sinners.

At the beginning of the Eucharistic celebration, through the penitential rite, the Church confesses the sins of the whole community and begs "blessed Mary ever-Virgin, all the Angels and Saints, and you, my brothers and sisters, to pray for me to the Lord our God." Intercessory prayer is a means and a sign of the intimate bond of communion that unites all Christians to one another. Through the voice of each of the faithful, the mystery of the Son who takes upon himself the iniquities of all the children in order to reconcile us all to God is renewed and perpetuated in the Church. While celebrating the Mass for Reconciliation in Seoul, Pope Francis reminded everyone:

> Jesus asks us to believe that forgiveness is the door which leads to reconciliation. In telling us to forgive our brothers unreservedly, he is asking us to do something utterly radical, but he also gives us the grace to do it. What appears, from a human perspective, to be impossible, impractical and even at times repugnant, he makes possible and fruitful through the infinite power of his cross. The Cross of Christ reveals the power of God to bridge every division, to heal every wound, and to reestablish the original bonds of brotherly love.
>
> This, then, is the message which I leave you as I conclude my visit to Korea. Trust in the power of Christ's cross! Welcome its reconciling grace into your own hearts and share that grace with others! (Homily, August 18, 2014)